Workshop of the
Holy Spirit

Workshop of the Holy Spirit

An Invitation to Theological Education

Doug Strong *and*
Jess Bielman

CASCADE *Books* · Eugene, Oregon

WORKSHOP OF THE HOLY SPIRIT
An Invitation to Theological Education

Copyright © 2022 Doug Strong and Jess Bielman. All rights reserved. Except for brief quotations in critical publications or reviews, no part of this book may be reproduced in any manner without prior written permission from the publisher. Write: Permissions, Wipf and Stock Publishers, 199 W. 8th Ave., Suite 3, Eugene, OR 97401.

Cascade Books
An Imprint of Wipf and Stock Publishers
199 W. 8th Ave., Suite 3
Eugene, OR 97401

www.wipfandstock.com

PAPERBACK ISBN: 978-1-5326-8909-3
HARDCOVER ISBN: 978-1-5326-8910-9
EBOOK ISBN: 978-1-5326-8911-6

Cataloguing-in-Publication data:

Names: Strong, Douglas M., 1956–, author. | Bielman, Jess, author.

Title: Workshop of the holy spirit : an invitation to theological education / Doug Strong and Jess Bielman.

Description: Eugene, OR : Cascade Books, 2022 | Includes bibliographical references.

Identifiers: ISBN 978-1-5326-8909-3 (paperback) | ISBN 978-1-5326-8910-9 (hardcover) | ISBN 978-1-5326-8911-6 (ebook)

Subjects: LCSH: Theology—Study and teaching.

Classification: BV4020 .S85 2022 (print) | BV4020 .S85 (ebook)

11/02/22

Permissions

Contents

Acknowledgments

WE'RE GRATEFUL TO THE educators, mentors, pastors, lay leaders, academic colleagues, and friends who've poured their lives into ours and made this book possible. Our co-conspirators in theological education have included Estrelda Y. Alexander, Ted A. Campbell, Stephen S. Carver, Cole Dawson, Jane Donovan, Bob Drovdahl, Jolynn Engellant, David Evans, Luke Goble, Nike and Herman Greene, Derick Harris, Craig Hill, Steven Holt, Langdon Hubbard, Steve Khang, Scott T. Kisker, Ken and Deborah Koehn Loyd, Robert W. Lyon, Arnold Oh, R. Kendall Soulen, Cassie Trentaz, Sondra E. Wheeler, C. Ronald White, and particularly our students, who taught us and shared their stories with us. Special appreciation is expressed to John Harrell, Heather McDaniel, and fellow members of the Wesleyan Studies Seminar at Asbury Theological Seminary.

Introductory Letter

Dear theological students,

In 1675, a Lutheran pastor and educator named Philipp Spener set forth a bold proposal that theological schools should be "nurseries of the church" and "workshops of the Holy Spirit."[1] Spener's invitational metaphors of nursery and workshop call for theological institutions to be spaces of creative spiritual growth where God's people are empowered to engage in innovative ministry. Because Spener wrote during a time, the late seventeenth century, when the labor force was in the process of switching to mass production, he deliberately drew upon the highly valued but vanishing concept of a medieval workshop. The workshop image lifted up the importance of quality products made by master craftspeople and the passing on of trades through apprentices and journeymen and women who watched and worked alongside others.

In that earlier era, the continuance of a craft depended on the caliber of relationships developed in the workshop. The training of pastors, Spener believed, should incorporate a similar, careful attention to mentoring. Like Spener, we believe that relationships between student and teacher are at the heart of what it means to pass the church along to the next generation. "What you have

---

1. Spener, *Pia Desideria*, 103. For consistency, this book will use the rendering *Philipp Jakob* to represent Spener's first two names when they appear in the body of the text.

heard from me through many witnesses," Paul enjoined Timothy, "entrust to faithful people who will be able to teach others as well" (2 Tim 2:2).

Many scholarly books have been written about the dilemmas of our day, primarily for professors; other, more popular books are being written for pastors on the subject of the changing nature of the church. This book combines these purposes by contending for a symbiotic interconnection between church and academy. Both of us are ordained clergy and theological educators; we love the church and the schools at which we teach, and we've each launched new theological programs. One of us has formally been the student of the other, but we've also *both* been learners—apprentices and master craftsmen for one another. It's that type of relationship, along with the qualities of a theological workshop, that we want to offer to you. In this book, we will explore the metaphor of the workshop as a way to understand theological education, much like Spener did.

Alongside our invitation that you enter into the workshop metaphor, we will also provide some backstory into theological education. At the end of each chapter will be a few pages of historical background that engage the themes of our text. Backstories have emerged as a great cinematic genre in our time. From superhero movies to political thrillers, we love to see characters or situations in their current forms and to learn gradually about the history that led to a story's important moments. To use backstories in this way serves both to entertain viewers and to educate them. In the *Harry Potter* series, for instance, we observe Professor Snape's actions and try to understand his motives. Eventually—spoiler alert!—we learn the full story of Snape's character and personal sacrifice, as Harry reads Snape's memories to uncover information about the professor's brave role as a double agent. It is in this backstory device that we find out larger truths about Snape, about Harry, and about the entire good-versus-evil fight at Hogwarts castle. The revealed content from Snape's memories exposits his true motives and the terrible confines within which he has been trying to do good. It gives Harry an appreciation of the true cost of

Snape's awful journey—the backstory of Snape's incredible depth of character.

In this book, we intend to show you the "backstory" of your theological education. We will pull its memory to show how ministry training, though originally a collaborative enterprise, became an industry of tuition, grades, and accreditation. Our use of backstory comes with hopes that you can understand the true motives of theological education, examine the confines within which it is trying to do good, and gain an appreciation of the sacrifice and the journey of those who have invested in it.

Spener's relationally oriented images ("nurseries of the church" and "workshops of the Holy Spirit") were part of a larger critique that spoke against the Scholasticism of his day and later could be applied to the scientism that gained steam and overtook the structures of Western academic culture, including clergy education. Instead of heeding Spener's call, however, the rationalist legacy of most Protestant university-based theological training, coming out of the Enlightenment and the educational approach of the University of Berlin (following Friedrich Schleiermacher) and its successors, led to the system of formalized theological education that we have today. Consequently, the study of theology in recent decades has little that distinguishes itself from any other academic program such as sociology, business, or literature. While all fields of study have fascinating qualities, discerning the unique calling of God for ministerial work in the kingdom is not like just any other subject and cannot be prepared for merely by viewing programs in a catalog, weighing the cost-to-benefit ratio, or taking an introductory class to determine one's interest in the topic.

Research, writing, and individualized graded exams each have an important place in theological education, but they also represent the standardized expectations for every academic program of accredited colleges and universities. Even the typical college or seminary internship fails to capture the nuances of various ministry contexts, since many professors view experiences beyond the classroom as extraneous add-ons. Accreditation, degrees of mastery, and major programs of study can fall short of measuring and capturing the soul-working and compassion-building faculties that typified ancient methods of ministerial preparation, but which have been lost in the climate of modern academic culture.

Nonetheless, college, university, and seminary-based theological education remains the most effective way to train ministers and others for the church of today and tomorrow. Now more than ever, the church needs to be disciplined by the insights of the academy to challenge and support its task of equipping leaders faithfully for a complex, changing society. But it is becoming clear that the education of church leaders needs to occur in classroom settings that are different from those in its peer (academic guild) programs; settings in which learning is outside of the classroom, but convincingly integrated with it, provides students with experiences that will prepare them for tackling the ethical challenges of the world with the message of Jesus Christ.

That's where you come in. For decades, indeed for over a century, theological institutions have been slow in their response to the world and to the developing needs of the church. Complicating this dynamic is the reality that the church itself has also been unresponsive to the demands of the gospel in contemporary society and has failed to be nimble enough to speak a relevant message of hope for the world. But just as the church throughout its history has responded to the promptings of the Spirit, you and other rising theologians of your generation get to do the same today, and your education is crucial to your response to the emerging realities of a diverse, globalized world.

Here's the key: effective ministry doesn't start when you graduate from your theological program; it starts now, in your years of ministry preparation. We want to be clear: push yourself to be the best student you can be intellectually. Throw yourself into the academic endeavor. Learn the craft of theological study in the workshop of your institution. Study the Bible, its background, critical approaches, history, and how to do theological interpretation of Scripture. Allow yourself to be taught and shaped by the history of the church. Master the doctrine of the Trinity. Learn soteriology and sacramental theology and their impact on Christians throughout the centuries. Explore theologies across cultural lines. Memorize every date you can within your own tradition. Get a 4.0 throughout your academic study because the world and your ministry context require excellence. But do not expect these achievements to be the only things that will prepare you well for ministry in today's world. They are absolutely necessary, but they are limited.

To be students and instructors in the workshop of the Holy Spirit, you will need to take your profound academic training to the roads, streets, and alleys of the cities and towns where you reside. Your Christology, for example, has to be large enough for a new friend (perhaps someone you'll meet through your field of education) whose intellectual capacity has been forever altered by the continued trauma of marginalization, coping mechanisms, or addiction. Your ecclesiology has to be wide enough to imagine Eucharist being celebrated at a diner at one o'clock in the morning by what in Portland, Oregon, they call a "sisterhood of ladies." Your eschatology has to be firm enough for those moments when you see the kingdom of God clearly among people groups that the church has rejected. You need the classic theological writings of Augustine or Thomas or Julian or Bonhoeffer in your backpack as you encounter indigenous spiritualities. You will draw from sound pastoral-care theories as you listen without judgment to the stories of those dealing with self-harm. Some education needs to be gained in the classroom; some must come from outside of traditional structures; and some has to come from classroom settings that are different from how they have traditionally appeared.

To be a student who matures within the nursery of the church, you will need to engage the academic and field-education structures of your program fully while also spending your preparation years examining the boundaries of their effectiveness. It is good for you to do this examining. God will be there to catch you, often through your faculty and your peers. In their best moments, they will discern your questions and concerns, reconstruct what has been torn down through holy deconstruction, and help you to find the Spirit of the risen Lord within your experiences. God's call upon your life is profound, but it may need crafting. That crafting can only happen in the workshop of the Holy Spirit.

This book is best read in a community of teachers and students, scholars and learners—your workshop. It is our hope that this offering will help to guide your educational experience.

Yours as fellow laborers in the craft of theological study,

Doug Strong
Seattle, Washington

Jess Bielman
Portland, Oregon

1 ———————————————————————————

Apprenticeship

*Learning Theology and Ministry
in the Spirit's Workshop*

If . . . persons are to be called to the ministry they must be . . . trained in our schools and universities. May God graciously grant that . . . [these] schools would, as they ought, really be recognized from the outward life of the students to be . . . workshops of the Holy Spirit.

—PHILIPP JAKOB SPENER[1]

PHILIPP SPENER, ONE OF the founders of the University of Halle in Germany, a famous center for ministry education, insisted that theological schools could become "workshops of the Holy Spirit." This intriguing metaphor immediately piques our curiosity. What would create the conditions necessary for a school to be such a workshop? And what will assist you—as a person preparing to enter into theological education—to be eager to start this process of becoming a learner in a theological workshop?

---

1. Spener, *Pia Desideria*, 103.

It takes risk to enter into theological education, a willingness to sit under the spiritual guidance of others. But education for ministry is also exciting and energizing. Hopefully, you are reading this in the midst of a wider discernment process of living a life committed to Jesus Christ and his ongoing call to serve the world. Perhaps your calling has come through an intense experience that reshaped your life. It may have come to you as a growing impression from within that you can no longer ignore. Or perhaps it is simply the next, natural step of obedience to the God of the Bible.

Welcome to this mysterious and sometimes arduous path. You join a long history of those who have dedicated their lives to God. Calling to ministry is a unique faith journey that has been written about extensively through the pages of history. Your response to the call of God will be both like and unlike the paths of your peers, requiring both formal academic training and critical reflection on things like gifts, skills, and "fit." But a call to ministry is also birthed from deep within, wrestled out in prayer, and nurtured in the essential community of faith.

You may be reading this book as an assignment for class. But much ministry training takes place outside the classroom, and indeed, not all vocational paths lead primarily through courses, credits, and commencement ceremonies. Many professions take a different model called "apprenticeship," the passing along of skills and knowledge for a craft from master[2] to novice. The craft cannot be learned in any other way than through the hard work of the creative process, which requires a great deal of hands-on training under the direction of the lead craftsperson. In today's world, apprenticeships are still used for electrician and carpentry work, some engineering and healthcare professions, and the fast-moving

2. From the sixteenth through the nineteenth centuries in America, the term *master* carried an abhorrent meaning, since the word often referred to people who enslaved other people in an entrenched system of racialized oppression. In this book, we're using the term *master* in a completely different sense, to refer to the much older medieval concept of a master craftsperson who functioned in a guild with other tradespeople. The master in a workshop did not overpower those who studied with him or her; the master instead worked with learners as colleagues in the craft.

field of green energy. For each of these professions, some of the training is done in a classroom, but the academy only exists to prepare the worker for his or her apprenticeship outside its walls. Apprenticeship programs take years before a person is set loose to work on their own.

Apprenticeship is a quintessentially communal process. The student labors side by side with the master and other apprentices, working on the same set of tasks. The master's job is both to create the craft or product and to teach others to do the creating themselves. The various elements of the job are not completed in separate sessions. Rather, the training is non-compartmentalized, the workers communicate closely with one another, and the master gradually hands over more and more control and freedom to the novices as they grow in skill.

Contrast this with the elements of traditional higher education, which came of age at the height of the Enlightenment and consist primarily of courses of classroom study. The higher-education industry today (especially at research universities, which set the academic bar for other schools) has often facilitated minimal faculty–student interaction in favor of grant-producing scholarship or large teaching loads.

Theologically interested students face a daunting task: they must find appropriate training in higher education as a pathway to the fulfillment of their calling to Christian ministry. But sooner or later, they discover that theological schools are not immune to the pressures affecting all higher education. Not every theological school, for instance, has kept pace with the perceived needs of today's ministry-directed students. Sometimes, the academy has lifted up ineffectual and outmoded church models as normative, placed far too little stress on spiritual development and practical ministry, or paid inadequate attention to social contexts and ethical decision-making. When combined with mounting school debt and increasingly busy lives filled with obligations to family, job, and church, pre-ministerial students often experience a disconnect between their interests and the theological education they have typically received.

Seminaries and college religion or theology programs continue to be exceptional places to prepare for a life of Christian service;
they really do remain the best option for ministry training. But
these dissonances create unnecessary barriers between students
and the full treasures of theological education. In addition to the
hard work of simply discerning their callings, theological students
feel that they also have to navigate the immense challenge of making sense of educational processes and curricula. "Is my theological
education relevant?" students today often ask. "Is it worth the cost?
Is the credentialing even necessary?" Meanwhile, the faculty and
administration of theological schools face similar questions, but
from the perspective of institutional sustainability and usefulness.

The modern (Enlightenment) model of higher education is
not like the life-on-life apprenticeship of a medieval workshop. But
many examples of theological education today are moving back in
the direction of what we argue is the rounder, healthier model of
a workshop. Think of professors who are holistically engaged in
ministry *and* in the lives of their students at the same time. Think
of students who sit with instructors working out a morning message for a congregation. Think of students who go along with their
faculty on hospital visits or to neighborhood association meetings.
Think of the breaking down of institutional structures that typically separate the lives of professors and students, so that it becomes
more common for students to interact closely with faculty at times
and places other than just in the classroom. The writer of Hebrews
addresses the process of engaging the education of leaders, particularly in the areas of character and faith: "Remember those who
led you, who spoke the word of God to you; and considering the
result of their conduct, imitate their faith" (Heb 13:7 NASB).

For centuries, even before the workshop model developed,
religious vocations were passed along in a monastic community
of learners and teachers who prayed, studied, worked, and lived
together. Abbeys, monasteries, and nunneries still bring in no-
vitiates for learning and discernment today, assigning novices to
mentors who support them in discerning the long commitment
that monastic vows demand. The community shares the daily

practices of life together and also acts as training for the everyday spiritual work of prayer and service. The role of the mentor is one of wisdom, careful questioning, and modeling.

Martin, now known as Brother Anthony, entered into an Anglican friary several years after completing a college religion program. Reflecting back on the nature of his classroom theological education in relation to his novitiate process, he attests to the power of apprenticeship at work in the development of his vocation. "In the one year I have been here," he says, "I can count on one hand the number of times my novice guardian [mentor] or others have sat me down to instruct me on 'this is how we do it.'" Instead, he says, the learning process is mainly to "sit next to me and do it with me." Reciting the daily morning prayer or serving San Francisco's homeless, Brother Anthony's experiences are deepening the spiritual and theological ideas he studied in college. Theology, he said recently, doesn't become effective until it "hits the road." Theological constructs "are just theories, okay in their own right," but they ultimately fall short of being fully adequate for preparing a person for ministry. The analogy that Brother Anthony uses to describe his current situation is that his formal theological training built a bridge, but his monastic experience allows him to walk across it. "I needed the dialogue of both of them," he says.

Brother Anthony is in a vocational–theological–educational discernment training that may take seven to ten years of "sitting next to me and doing it with me." All of the students in his monastic house are both participants and learners in the monastic life. The living and educational environment does not consist merely of teachers and students, with the novice guardian providing oversight. It is much more communal than that. "I am a student of the history, spirit, and rhythms of a movement," says Brother Anthony, "along with hundreds of brothers worldwide, a movement that dates back to St. Francis." He is a learner in the expansive network of ideas and practices of monastics throughout the centuries. He would not consider himself just a member of the monastic house or a follower of the novice guardian, but a part of a global movement within the wider church. Most of you will not be engaged in a monastic or intentional community like Brother Anthony. But all students within the workshop of the Holy Spirit will do well to find environments for ministry apprenticeship that can only happen in tandem with their peers and their teachers—that is, to work alongside a community of theological craftspeople.

Apprentices learn from experts over time, acquiring particular sets of skills along the way. The training is rigorous and exacting, and masters expect excellence, since the master's name will appear on the finished product. Likewise, apprentices in theological education must receive a rigorous and exacting education. The disciplines of biblical interpretation, our global Christian heritage, theology, and ethics provide the foundation. Your faculty teach these classes with excellence: the courses will be academically rigorous and will challenge your intellectual capacities, requiring you to develop your reading, writing, logic, and communication skills. But the curricula are also designed to elicit a sense of connection between the various courses and your life experiences. Push yourself to rise beyond basic academic expectations by going further than is asked in your classes. Theological education is a unique opportunity. You are probably paying a lot for it! You must learn the skills of the craft of ministry, both intellectual and practical, so as to become a high-quality craftsperson. Our Master's name is reflected by what you produce, so what you produce must be excellent: highly skilled biblical and community exegesis; a thorough knowledge of the church's tradition; doctrinal precision; theological proficiency; application of our triune God's character to the complex ethical issues of our day; well-delivered sermons; sensitive pastoral care; and emotionally intelligent interpersonal relations. Apprentices will also make mistakes, of course. But the workshop is just the place for those mistakes, for trial and error, to happen.

In the Pastoral Epistles, Paul provides a biblical example of apprenticeship when he advises Timothy to be strong and confident and to pass along his ministry to others. "What you have heard from me through many witnesses," he says, "entrust to faithful people who will be able to teach others as well" (2 Tim 2:2).

Paul is anticipating four generations of discipleship. He directs Timothy to find reliable people who can teach the generation after those he teaches. The line of legacy goes from Paul to Timothy, from Timothy to the faithful people, from the faithful people to their students, and—hopefully—onward through history as the process continues. In this education cycle, a new group of disciples have been instructed by the past and are a part of a process that is designed to endure and to grow across time.

Theological students today are eager for this kind of spiritual apprenticeship. Mentoring, one form of apprenticeship, offers a way for theological educators and pastoral leaders to invest in the next generation. It provides a window into the lives of those who are already serving the gospel of Jesus Christ. For many millennial and Gen Z students, fractured relationships have been the norm throughout their lives, and the curated images that they find on their peers' social media platforms can produce a sense of inadequacy and a pressure to keep up by appearing successful, resulting in an unceasing anxiety in daily life. Good mentoring can counter these negative images by helping mentees to calibrate their expectations to the grace of God instead of to the pressure of others. When a mentor listens well and is authentically available and vulnerable, the mentor reminds her or his mentees of the deep need for community and of the truth that they can actually experience dependability in relationships.

What is this generation looking for in mentoring? Rather than a prescribed set of principles, values, or virtues, theologians-in-training often want help in figuring out their purpose in life—their storyline. The toxic narratives that others have tried to impose on their lives can be reformatted so that they recenter their stories in light of God's narrative. Often, when theological students are well mentored in this way to see themselves as part of God's larger story, they in turn become excellent mentors who are "able to teach others as well."

How does theological apprenticeship appear within the workshop model? The workshop of theological education, if it remains open to the creativity of the Holy Spirit, will be a place where students will receive a holistic approach to church leadership training. They will develop skills and instincts for transformational experiences that supplement the reception of informational learning. They will choose inclusive collaboration instead of competition. They will desire to enter into paths of growth in holiness of life. They will acquire the ability to learn about various contexts and listen to them deeply. They will make space to receive practical ministry training. And they will engage with guides who are interested in drawing out their callings alongside their careers.

Transformational Experiences with Academic Learning

The academic content of informational learning is absolutely vital to effective ministry. Convictions in ministry are often birthed in the pages of a profound text, the deep examination of class assignments, or the nuances of approaches carefully scrutinized within a lecture. As theologically trained ministers,[3] we will forever take the insights we receive from Karl Barth's *Church Dogmatics*, our meticulously exegeted biblical texts, and our ethics papers with us to every meeting, every hospital call, and every pastoral care session. The Spirit of God is working within our classes and courses to shape the way we process the world and those we encounter. Our papers and exams become greater than assignments; they become experiences. These transformational experiences are the return on the investment we make with our higher-education dollar. These types of academic learning are profound because they intersect with our lived experiences of beauty and pain. The reading, writing, and lectures become more than academic variables: they become foundations upon which we build our lives in ministry.

3. We use the term *minister(s)* throughout this book in a broad sense that includes but is not limited to ordained clergy. Ministers are individuals vocationally engaged in all forms of Christian service, such as chaplains, pastors, seminary and college professors, Christian nonprofit and parachurch professionals, etc. And in an even broader sense, those of us who are heirs to Martin Luther's Protestant belief in the priesthood of all believers assert that every Christian is called to some sort of "ministry."

Reading, writing, and lectures, however, represent just a partial set of the experiences that God uses. Countless formative moments take place outside of the typical classroom setting, becoming part of our apprenticeship with the Spirit every bit as much as the academic experiences do. The church and the classroom are set up on the premise that we live differently because of convictions we hear or read—that we think our way into new ways of living. But much of the time, we *live* our way into new ways of *thinking*, a pattern that is often called the action–reflection pedagogical model. To engage with complex phenomena alters how we live and process information. When Timothy, a senior theology undergraduate, was asked to tell prospective students which book had been most important to his studies, he replied that it wasn't a book at all. "It was the field experiences I had with ministries in the city," he said, "that changed the way I read every textbook in the program after that."

Transformational experiences cannot be forced. There can be no "best practices manual" for creating or having them. But we do know that the strongest experiences of learning come from cognitive dissonance—from purposeful dislocations. These experiences include engaging others' pain until we arrive at a place of empathy, and engaging cross-culturally until we arrive at a point of questioning our assumptions. They include urgent moments that test decision-making and stretch us to the edge of our emotional limits in order to help us learn about boundaries. They shape the ways we understand the call of God on our lives. They change the way we see Jesus' interactions in Scripture and mark how we view the potential of the church. When engaged mindfully, these cognitively dissonant, formative experiences are not spiritually dangerous, simply because of the encouraging and caring community that theological education fosters. Allow yourself to get outside of your comfort zone, and let the supportive community around you catch you when you feel vulnerable. Such an integrated approach to theological education becomes a "nursery for the Church," to use Spener's phrase.[4] These are the moments when leaders are

4. Spener, *Pia Desideria*, 103.

born and church identity is shaped. They create a more just, holy, and dynamic church.

Tragedy struck Warner Pacific University several years ago when a beloved student suddenly died of an undiagnosed heart condition in the presence of his peers. While the campus community reeled in the days that followed, staff from the student affairs office gathered around those closest to the student, and some faculty put aside their usual schedule in the days following the tragedy to create the necessary space for processing. A class of ministry majors, in particular, instinctively began to act as caregivers around the campus, even while they themselves grieved. The ministry students also shared during their class time, telling stories of how they were balancing their own internal struggles while remaining supportive to those around them. They were engaging their fellow students even as they wrestled with their own thoughts and emotions. Students preparing for ministry need to learn the skill of caring for others while handling their own grief.

The juxtaposition of being in a ministry-preparation class while navigating ministry on campus was not lost on one student named Hailey. She pointed out that dealing with one's own emotions while dealing with others' feelings seemed like an essential aspect of the ministerial vocation in which she was engaged. Both practical ministry skills training and academic study (theodicy, for example) suddenly became extremely relevant. The conversations in class turned from processing into strategizing. The class began working together to determine who among them were so close to the situation that they simply needed to receive care; which of them needed regular check-ins as they balanced their emotions with the task of engaging others; and which of them had the emotional capacity to be a resource to their peers. This was collaborative and transformational learning in real time. The "walking-beside" Holy Spirit—the true Master of the workshop—seemed to be working in those moments to minister comfort to students even as they learned how to minister to others.

Collaboration Instead of Competition

Competition is alive and well in theological education as institutions scramble among themselves to woo students. The forces of competition regularly play out in the classroom as well. Most higher education in the West is based on an individualized scaling system, with standardized grading sometimes pitting students against one another. In spite of the best intentions of faculty, students perceive that formal grades create a hierarchy based upon a series of transactions. Fortunately, most theological schools have developed their curricula based on educational theory that recognizes multiple intelligences and ways of learning. Group work, for instance, is viewed as necessary. While some classroom rubrics tend to lift up linear, information-based learning, the church as described by Paul celebrates a variety of giftings needed for the work (1 Cor 12:7). Intellectual prowess, critical thinking, and analytical ability are each crucial, but they cannot be the only measures of success, especially for ministry. Ministers need the necessary individual skills of biblical exegesis and theological construction, but those must be exercised within community contexts that challenge assumptions. Ministry preparation settings can train students in this way.

The good news is that ministry is awesome! Sure, it's risky and dynamic, but that simply means that at its best, ministry will be collaborative, in order to encourage you through the times of challenge. Correspondingly, ministry training in a workshop of the Holy Spirit ought to be more collaborative than competitive. (There is enough competition in the church world already, given the pressure for flashier worship services, bigger buildings, and ever-increasing attendance numbers.) Some of the richest ministry settings are creative, collaborative environments that bring out a diversity of skills and perspectives, the sort that is needed for faithful presence in people's lives and communities.

Kyle came to his theological education saddled with a learning disability, dyslexia, which had gone undiagnosed through his early educational years. Despite his insecurities, he pushed into college with a sense of his call to ministry. He had internalized that he was "not book-smart" and often lamented to others how "dumb" he was next to his classmates who excelled at socialized educational activities. But when he entered into his ministry field education course, he found that its practical approach was far more conducive to his learning than traditional styles of course instruction had been. Along with others in the class, he visited several vastly divergent, nontraditional sites for ministry. The students, traveling in groups of three, developed skills of flexibility and openness to others. Kyle was no exception: through these experiences, he discovered ministry proficiencies both within the small groups and within the larger class dynamic.

Kyle discovered that he has unique ministry gifts that a standard classroom cannot measure: he is highly adaptable and competent in new environments, and he puts others around him at ease because of his personality strengths. Kyle spent his junior year of college listening to and assisting students who struggled deeply to engage these new and unfamiliar ministry settings. He became a leader in the field education course because of his natural relational skills and flexible personality. His gifts made him the best ministry collaborator of the class.

Kyle's ministry goals have never included becoming an individual minister at a large church. Rather, he has a heart for the marginalized within American society, and he easily makes friends across social barriers. Kyle sees his vocation as an organizer and collaborator for the good of his neighborhood, a vision that was shaped and formed by a participatory curriculum that ventured away from traditional methods.

Holiness of Life

In the epigraph at the beginning of this chapter, Philipp Spener addresses the "outward life of the students." In effect, by speaking about this outward life, Spener is stating that the person makes the profession—that character, personality, and convictions drive the particulars of one's career path and trajectory. Your inward spiritual life forms who you are in your external actions. In ministry, this is a very important dynamic. Your experiences with the divine are the source of both joy and pain in your ministerial call. The God who is invisible, and who sometimes seems silent, nonetheless accompanies you on the ministerial journey. Your path will be marked by your increasing capacity to discern God's voice, to discern God's silence, and to leap into the faithful unknown. Most counseling programs require that candidates receive many years of therapy for themselves. Similarly, your own spiritual formation may be the most important aspect of your ministerial life, though it will rarely show up on a transcript. "Faith," said Helmut Thielicke to theology students in 1962, "must mean more to us than a mere commodity stored in the tin cans of reflection or bottled in the lecture notebook, whence at any time it may be reproduced in the brain."[5]

Some family members or your church community may have warned you that you can lose your faith through your study of theology—that "seminary will become cemetery." Others may have suggested that you park your spirituality outside during your theological education, in order to quarantine your spiritual life and protect it from harm. Be wary of suggestions that you keep your life of faith unchanged and separate from your education during these years. Integrate your spiritual life and your study, rather than compartmentalizing them. Well-meaning advisors may tell stories of when an analysis of the Bible or of systematic theology led to a faith crisis or a sense of spiritual burnout. But this minimizes the Spirit's power to break in and shape your training and assumes God's distance or absence from the vital process to which God has called you. If theological schooling is a workshop of the Spirit, then God's Spirit is intimately and immanently present. God enters directly into your theological education years. The ideas and concepts that you encounter, no matter how challenging they might be, are means of grace. God is using the vast history of the church and the tradition of faithful souls who have come before us to be our guides. Theological differences—you will notice them in classmates, professors, and the curriculum itself—can serve you well as you struggle and learn. As you approach it reverently, the process

5. Thielicke, *Little Exercise*, 32.

will serve to solidify some ideas while breaking you of the need for certainty with other ideas. Let every concept, every piece of information, every experience that feels disjointed be a point for prayer and community. This is what Paul means when he admonishes us to be "transformed by the renewing of your mind" (Rom 12:2).

A young man named Seth found his life turned around when he experienced the good news of Jesus. God changed Seth's life so profoundly that he felt called into ministry. Seth matriculated at his undergraduate school full of expectation, but he soon discovered that he had reservations regarding the theology of some of his professors, a situation that many theological students face. The educators he encountered built their curriculum on ideas that seemed to run counter to some of the core convictions of his faith. Nonetheless, Seth jumped in with both feet and learned to trust the Spirit (through his professors) as he searched for truth. He describes the experience as "a formative but dark time." He regularly struggled with the nature of truth while negotiating the differences between his formative theological convictions and the conclusions of those around him. "How do we believe in such different things?" he asked. "Not everyone can be right, can they?" Seth dealt with his struggle prayerfully, and he came to realize that he had to engage the process and even the faculty with whom he disagreed. He often asked himself, "Seth, is there a chance you don't know better than these people?" The wrestling in his spiritual life, he recalls, resulted in "a killing of my pride" and "losing my life to save it." He continued: "I wanted to disagree humbly. You have to learn how to engage theological difference in order to disagree with it."

Seth's experiences motivated him into further theological study in graduate school. He describes his time in both his undergraduate and his graduate studies by saying his beliefs "were exploded, destroyed, put back together, and then exploded again." Each cycle reoriented his categories and taught him that truth is complex and fresh. Yet Seth never reconciled a few foundational pieces of his theology with the thought and experiences he encountered as an undergraduate. So how does he evaluate his collegiate theological education? "The core to my faith remains," he says, "but now it is better explored." Seth called upon the Spirit at points when his theological education got difficult and confusing. He was able to lean on his experiences with God, who used his theological training to shape his spiritual life. When you get to the end of the formal part of your theological education, you may find, like Seth did, a renewed vision of the convictions that formed you. Alternatively, you may find yourself in a different theological or social place from where you started. The most important concern is that you have faith that the Spirit will be walking beside you all along the way.

Your experiences with God will fuel your own relational and moral life during this season of study. Ethical integrity is absolutely essential for anyone entering into ministry, though questions of personal morality are frequently put aside during the period of one's theological education, a sequestering that is not healthy. This is not to advocate a legalistic, moral form of holiness. The holy life is not measured by a list of dos and don'ts, but by a heart directed toward God that results in loving God, neighbor, self, enemy, stranger, and earth. We must live into the high calling of serving as examples of faith, living in freedom from the legalistic expectations of others.

Spener, along with the pietists of his day, was worried that the pursuit of intellectual paths alone might cause one to lose the fundamental necessity of developing as a whole person, of growing deeply as a disciple of Jesus. You cannot be a fragmented person, someone who is one way in religious settings and another way outside of them. This fragmentation is very prevalent among churchgoers and is difficult to overcome. Our identity is shaped by the renewing love of Jesus in our lives. It is axiomatic that you should make decisions based on the times and directives when you hear God most clearly: "Believe in the darkness what you have seen in the light."[6] Your theological education is most likely a "one-time shot" that you have for engaging in the intensive study of God, the Bible, and those before us who have pursued God in their time. Let your convictions and the inner life of the Spirit integrate with each aspect of this learning. The result of your integration will be

6. Trotter, diary, August 10, 1901.

demonstrated through your relationships, sexual ethics, politics, food choices, downtime, use of money—indeed, in all that you do. When this devotionally grounded "outward life of the students" becomes evident, then, as Spener wrote, theological schools will be recognized as "nurseries of the church" and "workshops of the Holy Spirit."

Learning to Listen to Context

"Healthy study attends to life in the sense of mindfulness, of paying attention both to the subject matter of our studies and to the broader contexts in which our learning takes place."[7]

There was a time when missionary Christianity attempted to convert non-Western peoples to Western cultural ideals just as much as it tried to convert them to the gospel of Jesus Christ. They conflated Christ with culture. "The missionary impulse, which is the very heartbeat of the Christian religion," said the great spiritual writer Howard Thurman, "reveals to what extent a religion that was born of a people acquainted with persecution and suffering has become the cornerstone of a civilization and of nations whose very position in modern life has too often been secured by a ruthless use of power applied to weak and defenseless peoples."[8] This inability to contextualize the gospel has done untold damage to peoples and cultures. In more recent years, thankfully, many practitioners of the faith have learned to listen and to engage contexts. The posture of imposing the gospel on people and places has evolved into a posture of attending to the Spirit that is already at work within people groups and places. The need for contextualization is not just for overseas missions work anymore. It is a necessity for all ministry. One reason theological education is so powerful is that not only can it be transferable from one context to another, but it also requires a thorough knowledge of other contexts and a

7. Bass and Briehl, *On Our Way*, 25.
8. Thurman, *Jesus and the Disinherited*, xix, 2.

lot of humility. Thinking about and applying ministry in ways that are transferable require a specific set of skills.

The first tasks of engaging neighborhoods in cities or small communities are listening and learning. The Trinity is already at work in the lives and communities that we encounter, endlessly moving to enact God's redemption story. The work of the Holy Spirit began long before we began engaging ministry in a particular place and will continue long after we leave. Our invitation is to dive in and find where the Spirit is at work.

Our particular context, for instance, is the Pacific Northwest. Our region is viewed by many as a religious frontier. Christian entrepreneurs from other regions, seeking the vast land of unchurched people, move west in hopes that their ministry models will produce the types of church growth that succeeded in other parts of the country. Frequently, however, these impresarios discover that what worked elsewhere doesn't seem to translate well to Northwestern cultural spaces. They lament that "seminary did not prepare me for this."

Evidently, we need to understand the contexts in which we will be ministering. Effective theological education will assist us in developing those skills. Ministry classes that focus primarily on strategies, programs, or steps-to-a-process will likely serve a narrow cultural demographic of the school, its region, or the faculty member. This kind of focus may not be the most helpful type of training for those going into cross-cultural settings. Dominant-culture students may find that the strategies that seem common sense or the "right" way are actually culture-bound values. An example of this skewed emphasis on common sense strategy took place during the 1970s when some theological schools taught their students to follow the "homogenous unit principle," which stated that churches tend to grow when congregations are filled with people who are similar to one another. While sometimes true, this strategy did not work in places that valued multiculturalism (not to mention its implicit racism, or the religious fallacy of concentrating on only one group of people!). Such kinds of teaching may do more harm than good when applied outside of one's region of the country, racial group, or socioeconomic setting. Instead, ministers trained in the workshop of the Holy Spirit will learn to exegete communities. Like the exegesis of Scripture—the process of critically examining biblical passages, identifying cultural background issues, authorship, themes, and other factors that make up the creation of the text—the same care can be given to one's study of a place and people. Background issues, influences, events, and injustices often make up the "soul" of a place. It is important for those who are called to minister to become disciples (learners, apprentices) of those who have been committed to a place and people for long periods of time.

Estrelda Alexander entered into theological education in midlife. Having been a successful minister in the Washington, DC, area for many years, she enrolled at Wesley Theological Seminary to receive formal training. Finding her to be an impressive student, the Wesley faculty urged Estrelda to go on for her PhD, and she stayed local and finished her doctorate at the Catholic University of America. She went on to take administrative and faculty assignments at different theological schools. But during all this time, Estrelda perceived a significant, unmet need that engaged her academic journey and the context of her lifelong ministry. From her own background, Estrelda saw the lack of formal theological education options within the Black Pentecostal ministry context. She had learned from the few Black professors in her predominantly White programs, but nothing existed that focused on practical training for the Black church experience.

Estrelda heeded her calling into this need and founded William Joseph Seymour Foundation. The foundation is committed to strengthening the church by training leaders to engage in issues facing the Christian community. Estrelda's education uniquely prepared her to perceive and respond to the needs of her context. She understood her call to leadership and did not wait for someone else to do the needed work. Her faith and courage facilitate a legacy for her education that benefits the church and the rising leaders who serve it.

Practical Training for Ministry

Cultural exegesis is a skill. Various skills come naturally to some students, while others struggle to learn. Many so-called soft skills, such as emotional intelligence, are necessary for ministry but are rarely evaluated by a grade; they may take a different type of educational experience to build. Compassion, setting aside prejudice, and becoming sensitive to the promptings of the Spirit require experiential learning that cannot be fully grasped by a lecture or examined via a midterm.

Listening, perhaps the greatest ministry skill that can be learned and practiced, is a prerequisite to many ministry functions. It takes prolonged listening to exegete a community, to listen to the people and places that make it tick. It takes intentional listening to engage another's story enough to develop compassion. It takes the slowing down of our heart and mind to learn to listen to God. This availability goes beyond simply being a "good listener." A good listener refrains from talking over others and creates space when it is needed. The type of listening essential for ministry is a pursuit of proactive listening—an intentional quest to learn as much as possible about others while bringing one's authentic self to the relationship.

Voices of those who are different can be our best teachers. We do not always have the space or time in our classrooms to work out differences. The processes of community building, church staffing, worship planning, running nonprofit boardroom meetings, and collaborating in ministry all produce differences that matter. Navigating them is a practical skill. It begins with the proactive listening that profoundly shapes the community spaces that we create. In the short text he wrote as a manual for his underground seminary during the Nazi era, Dietrich Bonhoeffer called out the importance of listening as a ministerial act. "The first service that one owes to others in the fellowship," he wrote, "consists in listening to them. . . . So it is [God's] work that we do for our brother when we learn to listen to him. Christians, especially ministers, so often think they must always contribute something when they are in the company of others, that this is the one service they have to render. They forget that listening can be a greater service than speaking."[9]

Listening is also crucial for responding to crises. Many first-time ministers have lamented that their ministry courses could not have prepared them for the person who walks into their office in a present moment of unspeakable pain. Ministers cannot be experts on every human condition they may encounter. However, ministry trainees can be given opportunities to engage with individuals who are facing dire circumstances.

Theodore had a field education experience designed to create listening, empathy, and skills to engage with crisis situations. On Monday nights, he and other students interviewed people who were in the midst of some very tough life situations. Topics of these interviews ranged from drug addiction, pornography, sexual abuse, coming out to one's faith community, and suicide intervention. The field education supervisor made sure that students came with questions prepared, with an express prohibition against offering any quick solutions to the situations.

In the second week of the experience, Theodore followed all the rules by being attentive to the situation. The topic for the evening was suicide, and the speaker, a minister to first responders, talked about the frequency of suicide attempts among police officers, firefighters, and those in caregiving professions. He provided information on specific signs that indicate suicide risk, such as disturbing patterns of behavior. He also explained the need to ask direct questions of an at-risk person. He told Theodore's group to get past their own sense of awkwardness: "It is about the welfare of the other person," he said, "not about you." As a responsible educator, the speaker made sure that neither Theodore nor any of the other students believed that they were now experts in suicide intervention. They were told that their obligation was to refer. Nonetheless, Theodore was particularly attentive because of people in his own life who had committed suicide.

Five days later, Theodore went to visit friends and family. Never did he realize he would be called upon to use his newfound

9. Bonhoeffer, *Life Together*, 97.

knowledge so quickly. Theodore had identified some patterns of behavior in his mom, who had been open to him about her depression. "She was in a strange place that, prior to the time with the speaker, I could not identify or engage," he says. Moreover, "even if I could have identified suicidal behavior, I didn't think I would have asked the direct questions I needed to." Theodore overcame the awkwardness and asked his mom a direct question about possible suicidal intentions that he never wanted to ask or thought he could muster the courage to ask.

Theodore's use of the Monday-night training did not stop there. That evening, visiting his church, he noticed similar signs in a friend. "She was also in a depressed state," he says, "and I asked her a direct question about her intentions. She said yes as well." Theodore referred both his mom and his friend to trained therapists. "I was able to immediately apply that session with the speaker during the weekend with my mom and those whom I love who are close to me. Before this session, I wasn't humble enough to ask the direct questions. It changed the way I look at suicide and depression. Obviously, I still don't understand everything, but it did strip away my pride so I could engage."

Theodore is not just a student at his school. He is a student within the workshop of the Holy Spirit—a workshop that includes his school and many others. He engaged a skills-based ministry curriculum that the Master Craftsperson allowed him to draw from right away. Theodore's attentiveness to his class and his subsequent attentiveness to those around him put him in the right place to engage positively with the needs of those he loved. This is theological education that matters.

Students in a workshop of the Holy Spirit will find themselves involved in community ministry alongside their theological education journey. This includes, but can go beyond, internships and field placements. Indeed, it may be most helpful if students' contextual education placements are outside of their comfort zones. Students can become apprentices in ministry contexts while their theological educators—faculty, active pastors, field education supervisors, clinical pastoral education supervisors, community developers—teach and hone the students' skills. But their most effective teacher will be the lead Master when they rely on the Holy Spirit.

Emphasis on Calling

In higher education, the return on investment is ultimately when one lands a job. Formal jobs in ministry include staff of churches, nonprofit institutions, higher education institutions, community organizations, and others. The discernment of job direction to go along with your degree includes but goes beyond the aspects of your personality that match well with the profession, the passions about an aspect of the work that captures you, or the connections that can get you an interview. It is a struggle to perceive the directions in which God is leading you, especially coming from One who requires fidelity to a vocational path but who often seems difficult to understand.

Missional or direct callings from God are significant; they require a test of our faith. We are asked to act upon a direction without, as Heb 11:1 points out, assurances or evidence. We follow God, who bids us to certain kinds of work and invites us to make changes even if we are unsure. This may worry parents, friends, or church leaders who have invested in us. Some will question the decisions you make based on the internal impressions that you receive. This is reasonable. They are looking out for your best interests. We need to balance the truths that convict us—to respond to the unique voice of the Spirit as it leads us while still testing the Spirit within the communities that are most invested in us.

A calling to ministry may include traditional roles such as church pastoring or mission work or serving at religious nonprofit agencies, but it may go beyond those roles. Theological students have a long tradition of schooling their professors with their imagination of the call of God on their lives and the variety of ways that they live out their callings.

Marissa is an alum of Seattle Pacific University. She pursued a major in theology because she felt it was what God wanted her to do. Her family's strong faith and church upbringing encouraged this call on her life. After graduation, her eye for issues of justice that disproportionately affect Black people in America led her to be a co-founder of the Seattle chapter of Black Lives Matter. The primary election season in 2015 was a contentious time. It was a time that was ripe for new voices to emerge within the national dialogue. Marissa and a colleague decided that it was the moment for their voices to be heard.

Inspired by her faith and the theological sensitivities she had learned in her education, Marissa spoke up in a way that became the center of national attention. In August, a large crowd waited to hear Sen. Bernie Sanders of Vermont, a candidate for the Democratic nomination for president, speak at Westlake Park, one of downtown Seattle's main public squares. As Sanders was preparing to speak, Marissa and her colleague took the stage and seized the microphone to address the audience. They wanted to raise awareness about the lack of attention the major presidential candidates had paid to life-and-death issues, such as the police killing of Black people.

In a blog post on Medium several months later, Marissa recounted the toll that the aftermath of that event and the subsequent media spotlight took on her life. "Caught up in my own self-discovery and in the recognition of the circumstances of Black people in America, I responded to what I felt like God was telling me to do," she wrote. "That was my only commitment, to say yes to the next thing God put before me." Marissa's faith, along with tools she received in her theology major, made her an activist.[10]

Many are called to ministry within a holistic career. In the past, the term *bivocational* has been used to describe a minister who gets his or her paycheck from a so-called secular job while doing ministry on the side. Today's students often do not categorize their work in these ways. A holistic life of ministry may wed together business and social good, teaching and living in the neighborhood, or homeless ministry and a digital communications career that includes skill in social media engagement. Students are finding themselves less called to a role and more called to

10. Johnson, "Good Day to Die."

a particular missional context, combatting a social ill or pursuing an evangelistic enterprise. It is within that ministry context that a career and its attending skills become vehicles for a life of ministry.

Backstory One—Medieval Workshops as a Metaphor for Theological Education

Philipp Spener, a devout German Lutheran minister, employed the image of a medieval workshop as a metaphor for effective theological education. His pious desire (*pia desideria* in Latin) was that the church be renewed through spiritually focused ministerial training modeled on the mentoring that an apprentice receives in a workshop. By 1675, however, when Spener wrote *Pia Desideria*, artisan workshops were already on their way out. During the late seventeenth century, and increasingly for the next two hundred years, factories supplanted small workshops. Mass production replaced the practice of producing quality crafts through the work process of mentoring and learning. In Spener's day, during the early stages of the industrial revolution at the start of what we now refer to as the modern era, manufacturing on a large scale arose as the accepted new method, since it was viewed as more efficient and cheaper than craft shops.

This alteration in the way that goods were made had enormous implications for everyday life. (Karl Marx was correct, at least in this aspect of his analysis, that change in the means of production affects the whole culture.) Spener wrote at a time, the beginning of modernity, when industrialism was displacing the workshop model. He derided the cultural implications of this change, for he observed raw competition over collaboration, laborers divorced from pride in their work, and assembly lines taking over from the process of masters teaching apprentices.

The changes in modes of production affected higher education along with all other kinds of vocational training. Universities, including their departments of theology, were modernized. But Spener preferred that the "craft" of learning theology should follow the former model of the workshop, and he favored the older mentoring method. He was even audacious enough to infer that the "master" who was doing the teaching for pastors-to-be was none other than the Holy Spirit.

The idea of a workshop was itself an innovation that developed five hundred years before Spener as an alternative to the feudal system. In place of serfdoms (a system whereby peasants worked for no pay at the behest of a feudal lord), a new system evolved in the twelfth century whereby young workers would become learners of a craft under the tutelage of a master who was an expert in that trade. These apprentices eventually became skilled and would become wage earners. Many of them progressed into becoming masters themselves.

The workshop represented the most distinctive feature of late-medieval urban society. The agrarian feudal structures that had been common didn't operate well for organizing the work of craftspeople, who lived in towns and cities. Young artisans began to learn their trades in the shops of master craftspeople. These tradesmen labored for themselves, producing their own goods and then selling them directly to the public. Apprentices, journeymen, and journeywomen worked for masters, who organized themselves into guilds.

The word *apprentice* was originally a French term, a contraction of the Latin *apprehendere*, as in apprehending or grasping a trade. An earlier Latin term for an apprentice was *discipulus*, which refers to someone who is a learner or pupil and is the root of the familiar English term *disciple*. An apprentice, then, is first and foremost a student. And conversely, a student is an apprentice—that is, one who apprehends what they're learning. Apprenticeship is a system in which the master is obliged to teach and the apprentice obliged to learn. By analogy, all of you who are students in theological education, in this "workshop of the Holy Spirit," are learners, are disciples. Learning defines one's apprenticeship in any craft, including the craft of studying theology.

In medieval times, the apprenticeship system allowed young men and women to acquire vocational education in various trades while supplying a workforce for thriving entrepreneurs.

Formal agreements, often in the form of contracts, were made between the master and the apprentice. The agreement required the apprentice to be trained for a specified period, from one year to as many as seven, after which the apprenticeship ended and the apprentice might become a journeyman or journeywoman, or eventually a master.

There were other requirements in such agreements. A common one, for instance, stipulated that apprentices were not allowed to marry; another one forbade them from running away from the shop. (Fortunately, theological schools today aren't that restrictive! You can marry while in school. We also suppose that you can even run away from your schooling—though we trust that you won't!) While the agreements had very specific obligations and reflected the high standards of the craft guild, they also left room for individual circumstances, allowing each artisan's shop to be shaped by the abilities and expertise of the master and to be altered according to the training needs of particular apprentices. We hope that you will find that your education, while adhering to certain commonly agreed-upon subject areas of theological knowledge and ministry skill sets, will also leave room for your unique circumstances.

While the majority of the craft workers were men, women took an active part in many of the trades as well. Women, for example, predominated in the trades of silk spinning, making women's headwear, and tavern and hotel management. Similar to the male "masters," these women achieved the official status of "mistresses."

Since the shops of master craftspeople were also their homes, the modern distinction between home and workplace, between private and public spheres of activity, between faith and work, did not exist. What has sometimes been referred to in modern society as "first place" (home) and "second place" (work) were conflated in medieval urban communities. This conflation of roles had huge implications for Christian ministry as well, and for how people were trained for ministry. In relation to one's ministry, for example, a person's home and family interacted in tandem with their calling. In Roman Catholic settings, priests, monks, and nuns frequently lived in community with one another. After the Reformation,

Protestant clergy included their families in their ministry. And in Spener's understanding of a theological community, faculty and students were to be in close proximity, so that "the students would have a living example according to which they might regulate their life, for we are so fashioned [by God] that examples are as effective for us as teachings, and sometimes more effective."[11]

Similarly, in the late-medieval ideal, theological communities did not separate their spirituality from cognitive theological argumentation. Affective and logical discourse coexisted seamlessly. The kinds of divisions that became common later in modernity did not predominate in medieval thought.

The blurring of various aspects of life—business life and domestic life, for example—functioned to women's advantage. A master's wife and daughters could learn the skills of the trade just like male apprentices. In fact, master craftsmen and their wives normally shared authority over apprentices, since the wife was well acquainted with her husband's craft. Widows often carried on the trade of their deceased husbands. Many women learned the trades.

In 1294, for example, a young woman named Marie who lived in Montpellier, France, wanted to become a trained seamstress, and so for a three-year period, she became the apprentice of a tailor named Mr. Durante. Marie agreed to be a clerk in training as a learner. Both Mr. and Mrs. Durante agreed to teach Marie the craft.[12]

While the term *apprentice* evokes the medieval guild-and-workshop system, some forms of this kind of work lasted through most of the industrial revolution. In fact, the status of a pupil or learner for vocational training remained into the nineteenth century in a few fields, and it remains in use in some fashion even today, particularly among specialized trades such as carpentry and electrical work.

Spener appropriated the image of the workshop for theological schools, but he did so just as the workshop system was waning. He recognized that the emerging modern form of university

11. Spener, *Pia Desideria*, 104.
12. Epstein, *Wage Labor*, 76–77.

training for ministry would be individually focused, competitive, and based on the retention and regurgitation of rationalistic content or critical thinking separated out from one's devotional life. He held up the metaphor of the medieval workshop because it represented ministerial training that was practical and collaborative, emphasizing quality, the holistic inclusion of both student and teacher alike, the integration of ministerial work with home and family, and the intertwining of spirituality with rationality. All of these concepts were being challenged by modern understandings of higher education, which was being transformed in Spener's day, just like all other ventures and social constructions. The changes appalled Spener. We have inherited the modern university system that Spener rejected, but his understanding of the workshop can be retrieved by theological educators today.

2

Craftsmanship

Forging the Story of the Gospel through
the Medium of Today's Context

IN MEDIEVAL WORKSHOPS, APPRENTICES, journeymen, and masters all labored together to produce high-quality artisanal goods. These goods represented a wide array of crafts, such as ceramics, shoemaking, weaving, glassblowing, upholstery, cabinetry, metal toolmaking (as with tinkers or blacksmiths), and many others. It was the responsibility of masters to pass the specifics of the trade onward to their apprentices. Masters taught those who came after them about the story of the craft, its lore, its narrative, its heritage and tradition.

Universities during that era began to apply a similar method to learning, as did the craft guilds. Students at universities learned a "profession," a field of study, in ways somewhat analogous to how one learned a trade. That is, comparable to apprentices learning under master craftspeople, university students learned under the tutelage of "professors"—expert teachers in their professions. The three recognized professions in the medieval period were medicine, law, and divinity, the study of ministry. When students acquired the requisite knowledge and skills for their profession, they became "masters," as in "masters of divinity," akin to the craft masters of a trade.

In the same way that craftspeople create a craft, a particular product, those preparing for ministry are also working on a product. What is the craft of divinity, the product of the study of theology and ministry?

The craft of ministry, and thus the responsibility of theological education, is the process of studying, and then proclaiming, the gospel of Jesus Christ. In the early church, such proclamation was known as the *kerygma*, the core teachings about Jesus: the message of Jesus' ministry and the announcement of salvation through his life, death, and resurrection. Passing onward the craft of ministry includes the gospel's narrative, heritage, and tradition: the story of Israel, Jesus, and the church. Our first task as theological educators—professors and students—is to master the content of the gospel and then learn how to share its profound message with others effectively. But effective sharing of the gospel can only take place if we clearly and lovingly comprehend the circumstances, background, and framework of the people with whom we're sharing it. That is, we must understand and interpret the context in which we're ministering.

Craftspeople must master the medium in which they are working (silver, iron, lace, etc.). The medium is the substance through which the craft is produced—the clay for a potter, for instance, or the wood for a cabinetmaker, or the fabric for a clothier. Similarly, as women and men in ministry, we must learn our medium well. Our context is the medium, or the substance, through which ministry is produced. Thus, we must become experts in knowing the context, or contextualization.

This chapter describes the craft of ministerial vocation—studying and proclaiming the gospel—in today's context. How does a student prepare well for Christian leadership in twenty-first-century cultures? How are changes in the world changing the church and therefore changing the ways that we minister? Not only will theological students need to be learners from experts who profess knowledge of ministry and the content of the message;

students (along with faculty) also need to reposition themselves to be dynamic co-learners with the church in the emerging world.

Applying Yourself: Your Training in the Craft of Ministry

Our craft is to learn and to proclaim the good news of the gospel. This *kerygma* is the truth to which we bear witness. As Karl Barth wrote, revelation is both "a radical teaching about God" and "the radical assistance of God."[1] The Bible and our theological traditions pass along the stories of our craft, while our convictions and ministry hopes are new and fresh to us. Whether we acknowledge it or not, we inherit our faith from Spirit-led people who have come before us.

While aspects of the craft of ministry change constantly, the *kerygma* has been passed on faithfully for two thousand years across the globe. We learn the craft of the *kerygma*, proclaiming the good news, from its heritage and traditions. "Living theological traditions," writes Lisa M. Hess, "promise a deeper way of knowing in community and its human frailty, given historical witness over centuries of God's people who have bridged texts and traditions too diverse to name."[2] In the sixteenth century, for instance, the Protestant Reformers determined that certain aspects of the faith that had been downplayed for hundreds of years were actually essential. These church leaders articulated doctrines such as *sola scriptura* and justification by faith alone. They also created a classification, known as *adiaphora*, for ideas and beliefs *not* essential to the foundational life of faith—matters of church doctrine or practice that are neither mandated nor forbidden.

Today, church bodies still argue about what things should be considered *adiaphora*—nonessentials for the faithful maintenance of the faith. In the workshop of your theological education, you will need to learn to discern what is *adiaphora* and what is essential for faithful proclamation. You will need to understand

1. Barth, *Church Dogmatics* 1.2:307–8.

2. Hess, *Artisanal Theology*, 28.

how to navigate situations of dispute and controversy. Often your theological education classroom can be the best place to test ideas, to explore different ways of thinking, and to engage in spirited disagreement about these classifications.

Theological education can be a place for exploring differences of belief, especially if you have developed an attitude of trust and mutual care with your classmates (we will say more about collaboration later in this chapter and in the next). In such a case, the classroom may function less like a checkout counter where you make the final purchase of your convictions, and more like a dressing room to try on ideas and look in the mirror. You may find that some ideas fit well or look good on you, while others don't. "My plea," wrote Helmut Thielicke to theology students, "is simply this: every theological idea which makes an impression upon you must be regarded as a challenge to your faith. [So] do not assume as a matter of course that you believe whatever impresses you theologically and enlightens you intellectually."[3]

In theological education, you must study and know the work of ministry—of proclaiming the message of Jesus for today. Like apprentices, students in a theological workshop must master their subject. You will probably not have the time to explore the entire depth of the mysteries of the Bible and all the richness of the church's traditions. This is your moment, however, to work hard, to be attentive, and to enter deeply into conversations to which you may never again have access. With the demands of life and ministry, you may not be able to take in everything about biblical studies, systematic theology, ethics, pastoral counseling, or any other theological subfield. Yet you will gain the most by taking these years of study seriously and pulling every bit of knowledge from the experience. This is the time and the space for you to nurture the life of the mind and to develop your intellect to its fullest capacity.

There are times when our education system rewards minimal effort: students can graduate, having "passed" their courses, but without excellence. Passing something by is not the same as taking it in. Professors rightfully become agitated when students

3. Thielicke, *Little Exercise*, 31.

approach class with the implicit question, "What is the least I can do to get the grade I want in the course?" This posture toward theological education often expresses itself as an expectation that the program of study is just a necessary hurdle to jump in order to obtain a degree that the student needs for credentialing. True, some students have complicated life situations that require them to make sacrifices for their education; for them, the demands on their time and resources impede their ability to be immersed fully in their theological study. But others miss the best that their education offers them for reasons that are entirely avoidable, such as a lack of maturity, an undisciplined life, or a confused sense of call.

Joseph grew up in various churches where his father was the pastor. In his Korean American household, he never really felt that he had an alternative but to follow in the family business. Everyone in his family and home church assumed that this eldest son would become an ordained minister. When Joseph came to seminary on a full scholarship right after his college graduation, he had little interest in his courses. He sat at the back of every classroom, playing video games. A two-hour class, he determined, provided almost the exact amount of time to watch a movie. When Joseph spoke up in class, he displayed a combination of caustic humor, cynicism, and sarcasm. He did not endear himself to his professors, nor did he really care.

Eventually, Joseph grew into the idea of ministry. He found himself as a husband, a father, and—yes, a pastor. When he happened to meet up with one of his professors some years later, Joseph apologized for his snarky, nonchalant attitude. "Now I wish I'd applied myself in my courses," he said. "What a lost opportunity!"

The Bible as the First Book of Instruction

The Bible is our chief resource for ministry training. We need it for the instruction of a life lived in service to the Creator. Many of the books of the Bible were written to be read aloud in community for instruction. Scripture's original method of encounter was not individual private reading for personal spiritual renewal, though it can be appropriated in that way. The Jewish communities would gather around for public reading, followed by conversation. Many of the stories were passed on through oral tradition within families and public discourse. Paul's letters in the New Testament were not written primarily for personal consumption. They were meant to be read in the house-church communities as stories and instructions to be discussed, lived, and distributed.

In theological education, the Bible is the first textbook of instruction in our program of study. We do not sell it back to the bookstore after our survey classes, because we never graduate from its ongoing ability to form us and to form our ministry vocation. Through "the revelation attested in Holy Scripture," Barth wrote, "we are struck to the very roots, to the heart. Our whole existence is called into question. . . . In revelation God tells man[4] that He is God, and that as such He is his Lord. In telling him this, revelation tells him something utterly new, something which apart from revelation he does not know and cannot tell either himself or others."[5] Through the Scripture, God claims us and shapes us.

The Bible remains with us in the life of ministry because our study in the workshop of the Holy Spirit is not primarily a degree to be earned. The Holy Spirit, through the Bible, continually teaches us the *kerygma* for our times. This *kerygma* is more than verbal telling. It is the proclamation that is spoken, lived, practiced in community, witnessed to through evangelism and in work for justice, and grown in faith communities.

The church's heritage and tradition are not ends in themselves. The church in every age wrestles with faithfulness to the *kerygma* in its context. Many ministry models have persisted across time but need to adapt to changes in context. In the Spirit's providence, the *kerygma* continues to thrive within various models and will remain into the next seasons of the church's history.

4. In this quote, Barth uses non-inclusive language to refer to all people. Although such language was normative when Barth lived and wrote, we acknowledge its inherent discriminatory nature.

5. Barth, *Church Dogmatics* 1.2:302, 303.

Learning and Knowing the Medium of Ministry

Medieval craftspeople knew that they needed to learn all about their medium, including the particular characteristics of the substance with which they worked, such as wood, metal, or cloth. In the craft of ministry, the world we live in is our medium. And the context for ministry is our *current* everyday life, not some future time when we may obtain a coveted leadership role. "Healthy study," writes Matthew Boulton, "attends to life in the sense of mindfulness, of paying attention both to the subject matter of our studies and to the broader contexts in which our learning takes place."[6] We are students of the Bible and tradition, living out the craft in the church and the world. But how do we negotiate the relationship of the church to the world? How do we proclaim the *kerygma* faithfully in complex times?

More specifically, how are changes in the world changing the church? And how are changes in the world and the church changing the ways in which we minister? And how do the changes in the ways we minister affect how we train for ministry? While you may be (rightfully) focused largely on the ministry needs of the present moment, it will also be helpful for you to understand what's been happening culturally since a decade or two before you showed up on the planet, not to mention the centuries of the church's history prior to that. We will discuss some of these cultural trends, the specific characteristics of our medium, and how they should have an impact on your theological education.

Going Small

An obvious cultural trend in the medium of our ministry today is the omnipresence of new technologies. The technological revolution of the past forty years produced a world that is more connected than ever before. We have unprecedented access both to knowledge and to one another. By browsing Twitter, we can get information as weighty as the latest breaking news from somewhere

6. Boulton, "Study," 25.

across the globe, or as trivial as the breakfast choice of a childhood friend we haven't seen in years. We have access to a vast amount of knowledge, claims, and worldviews. We can spend endless amounts of time mining the depths of untold quantities of topics. We're driven to consume more stories of interest or to explore an infinite number of subjects.

Humans are drawn, however, to more than the acquisition of information. People seem tied to screens that keep their eyes focused downward. Our ears are affixed with earbuds, keeping the sounds of the world around us at a distance. We are simultaneously connected and disconnected. We are tied more closely to those around the world whom we cannot access physically, but more disjointed from the people directly around us who are available to create community. We experience an increasing need for intimacy, but we have fewer interpersonal skills to achieve the relationships for which we long. In 2008, Sherry Turkle, an MIT professor and media theorist, wrote about the implications of personal handheld technology. "We are tethered," she wrote, "to our 'always-on/always-on-us' communication devices and the people and things we reach through them: people, Web pages, voicemail, games, artificial intelligences. . . . These very different objects achieve a certain sameness because of the way we reach them. Animate and inanimate, they live for us through our tethering devices, always ready-to-mind and hand."[7] By allowing our technological means to define our time, we miss connections that matter through relegating individual interactions to the same level as everything on our smartphones that competes for our attention.

In such a world, impersonal educational environments of large classes can seem comfortable. Church communities that are too large to pay attention to single individuals, who slip in and out of services, can seem convenient, or even preferable, for some people. But it's imperative that we move outside of our bubbles into a relational proximity that can't be achieved with even the best digital devices.

7. Turkle, "Always-On/Always-On-You," 122.

In many ways, our technological growth is a product of the modern theory of cultural progress. We are moving toward a bigger, faster, and more digitally connected world. Historically, the Western world has measured success by the degree to which we can grow our capacity. Churches have sometimes adopted that worldview as well. Before the Internet, many churches in the 1980s and 1990s hoped to maximize their impact by increasing their numbers of people, services, and programs. They achieved bigger capacity through demographic surveys and targeted media efforts. But as churches became more and more successful along those lines, they inadvertently made their congregations more and more impersonal as they transformed into "megachurches." This domineering term reflects the increased footprint of power that is achieved by large membership and budgets.

In light of the increasingly impersonal feeling that developed in very large churches, some congregations started cell-group ministries. They knew that disciples who want to grow experience a depth of spiritual engagement from knowing others and being known themselves. Such connections can never be relegated just to a subset program within the congregation's mission at large. Consequently, quite a few larger churches today are moving from program-based small groups to rediscovering various forms of relational ministry.

One can access the best preaching in the world through podcasts and YouTube. Church music in any and every form is available via streaming services. It's easy to donate online to charities or to activist causes. We can engage with many expressions of the Christian life through disembodied media, and the COVID-19 pandemic in 2020–2021 made streaming and Zoom services a necessity for many churches. God's real presence, however, and *your* real presence, are not digitally reproducible. The depths of your bodily companionship are not downloadable. The compassion of your touch is not a button on social media. Biblical authors could never have imagined the digital connectedness of our age. Scripture exhorts its readers to "wash one another's feet," "greet one another with a holy kiss," eat together, and "sing psalms and hymns and spiritual songs among yourselves."[8] Going small is going personal and intimate with significant in-person presence.

In many settings, going small is the new big. The impact of the *kerygma* is best received in life-on-life settings. The changing technology of the world has created some wonderful virtual resources for our life of faith, but it cannot replace the committed band of believers engaged with one another. The Protestant Reformers, Philipp Spener in the following century, John Wesley after him, Dietrich Bonhoeffer in wartime Germany, parachurch ministries of American evangelicalism, base communities in Latin America, and house churches throughout the ages have discovered that going smaller can result in a deeper sense of spiritual connection. "Community life cultivates receptivity for God's reign and also proclaims it," writes Gustavo Gutiérrez, the father of Latin American Liberation theology. "In this reception and proclamation a community builds itself up as a community."[9]

Christians are finding ways, both inside and outside of the church context, to achieve Gutiérrez's vision. House churches, neighborhood ministries, and ad hoc communities exist within the framework of churches and denominations, exemplifying ecclesial (church) expressions with greater relational connection. Our training for ministry needs to engage with these various structural changes and the implications of those changes for our theology.

Going Slow

Social media provides wonderful opportunities for us to share our lives. But what we share are only those aspects of our lives that we construct for social consumption. The picture that someone draws from social media is only a fragment of ourselves; consequently, social media can lead to the fragmentation of our lives. We can never be too careful about the person we portray online. Prospective employers, for instance, are looking at social media accounts

8. John 13:14; Rom 16:16; 1 Cor 11:33; Eph 5:19.
9. Gutiérrez, *Drink*, 134.

of applicants. Our ability to shape a version of ourselves carefully is creating interesting implications for our identity. Am I the person that I construct for others? Am I the person that I hide from others? Am I both? How am I to understand the complicated versions of me that surround me?

These questions become even more complicated when we try to understand others from their own social media constructions. People seem to assume a level of acceptable hypocrisy from the public images that others create. We assume an even greater level of acceptable hypocrisy from famous public figures. Due to well-publicized moral failings or co-opted political lives, for instance, we often look at major religious figures with suspicion. This level of hypocrisy and distrust becomes a challenge for the effective proclamation of the *kerygma*. We are trying to invite those outside the faith to trust in Jesus and his church while distrust of institutional religion is very strong.

"Going slow" is the new progress. Some of the most beautifully complex aspects of life are tough to measure. The health of a marriage, a life-giving friendship, and the joy of a good job are nearly impossible to capture in data or in tweetable mantras. Relational depth is essential for the Christian mission of *kerygma* to be received. "The primary work of Slow Church is not attracting people to our church buildings," wrote C. Christopher Smith and John Pattison, "but rather cultivating together the resurrection life of Christ, by deeply and selflessly loving our brothers and sisters, our neighbors and even our enemies. As we holistically embody Christ's love, we find joy that we pray will draw people closer to Christ."[10] Smith and Pattison suggest that the church cultivate the resurrection life of Christ rather than concentrate on converting people, since others emulate a life lived rather than an agenda foisted on them. This end goal is difficult to evaluate. But growth can be measured in many ways, only some of which are quantifiable. For example, the White North American church is "in decline" by the assessments of Sunday attenders or money given. (This is not the case, by the way, among congregations

10. Smith and Pattison, *Slow Church*, 33.

composed mainly of immigrant communities.) Nonetheless, one could argue that the church is growing in many ways. In some parts of the United States, almost no one attending church any longer is a nominal or cultural Christian; rather, those attending are dedicated disciples who want to be in church. That's growth! In the Pacific Northwest, it is sometimes quipped that the level of church participation compared to that in other regions of the US is similar to the region's famous espresso: smaller in quantity, but stronger. Indeed, it can be argued that the church in many places is growing theologically, ethically, and relationally. Such growth builds upon process, is highly relational, is spiritually alive, and is frequently slow. After all, patience, and not clout or power, is among the fruit of the Spirit. The fruit of ministry that Jesus refers to in John 15 consists of abiding in him and loving others. Loving and abiding are process outcomes with few measurables. We can see growth in kingdom work as we become increasingly comfortable with non-closure, imperfection, and experimentation. This product is relational, but it's also messy.

Perhaps slow can be the new progress in ministry training as well. Many of the processes of theological development can't be rushed or cut short. Due to rising tuition and time demands, more and more students choose not to matriculate into traditional, residence-based ministry degree programs. But doing so has a cost. Most schools see their theological education mission as more than curricular. Spiritual growth and vocational discernment are aspects of training that come from being part of the community and remaining in relationship with faculty and other students. The theological education journey can be stifled by being too busy or staying focused too far into the future. Students want to be active in ministry and to begin the work to which they are called. They need a balance of study and ministry. In most theological programs, students are involved in ministry work alongside their education. That ministry work, however, should not consume them to the point of neglecting the important opportunities of their education. Often this balance gets upset because classroom education and ministry experiences are disconnected. Students may already be involved in ministry and trying to do their education "on the side." Other students may be offered paid ministry roles during college or seminary that ask them to fill a need that seems unrelated to their student life.

Xavier came to his theological education program with an eager sense of call to ministry, a frenetic personality, and a fervent desire to engage with urban poverty. He took courses during his first two years of college that engaged his areas of passion. While his learning was relevant, it also served to increase the sense of urgency he felt to get out of the classroom and "do ministry." Xavier's struggle with this emerging impatience grew more and more consuming as his second year unfolded. He was caught between enjoying his education and becoming insatiably eager to live out the convictions about which he was learning. He felt stuck. The dilemma of being a full-time student left him feeling bifurcated. He voiced his frustrations to a few people who had little to offer him other than suggesting that he choose one or the other. He could throw himself at his education and be patient with his passions, or he could drop out of school to pursue ministry and lose out on the educational process that he savored.

Thankfully, just at that moment, his school was experimenting with "Living and Learning Communities," one of which provided Xavier with an outlet for embodied ministry while he was still engaged in his more formal theological education. The programs served as laboratories for Xavier and other students within the ministry training program to practice their spirituality, develop godly character, and serve in the neighborhood. The hands-on living component of ministry training seems obvious to students like Xavier. Students often experience the real demands of education while needing outlets for the type of learning that goes beyond exams and papers. Xavier decided that the slow path was the right path. He faithfully engaged both action and education.

Authentic Presence

Suspicion and hypocrisy result in a distrust of institutions and the erosion of authority. Government institutions and leaders frequently demonstrate failed promises. In 2015, the *Washington Post* reported on the distrust of institutions by the millennial generation. When surveyed, only three institutions scored over 50 percent on a trust scale, indicating that respondents had a "great deal" or "quite a lot" of trust in them. Congress and television news were at the bottom of the scale, while the military, small businesses, and the police were at the top. (We know, however, that even those institutions have recently been objects of distrust.) Organized religion ranked fourth on the list, with just 45 percent of respondents trusting it "a great deal" or "quite a lot." This statistic is not good news for the reputation of the church or those preparing to lead it. "Society-wide, trust in institutions is at or near record lows," wrote Chris Cillizza in the piece. "There is a feeling that the safety net is gone. In political terms, the conviction that honest brokers simply don't exist leads people to seek sustenance from those who affirm their points of view."[11] Such distrust did not begin with millennials or Gen Z. Generation X, just like the hippie movement of the 1960s and '70s before them, experienced cultural factors that similarly created cynicism.

Our North American context is our medium, and the erosion of authority influences the church significantly. The public is less trusting of leaders. We must navigate this culture of distrust, a bona fide challenge for those who aspire to leadership. Ministry leaders must be wary, for example, of setting themselves up as moral authorities. We are compromised by an ever-moving set of moral expectations. Our own failings are exaggerated when the spotlight is on. As fellow citizens who are concerned about the misuse of authority, rather than act defensively we should be present faithfully within the spaces we occupy. We have the opportunity to stand in solidarity with those who have been hurt by authority, especially religious authority.

In the 1990s and 2000s, congregations often held out cultural relevance as a goal as they related to the world around them. Some churches made attempts at mimicking popular culture with their music and their programs in an effort to make people feel more

11. Cillizza, "Millennials."

comfortable with their church experiences. Church architecture drew on business and entertainment modes for the creation of space, so that church buildings came to resemble movie theaters in office parks. Church services drew on media patterns to appeal to non-Christian audiences. But that created its own set of problems. "Chasing cultural relevance," Karl Vaters reminds us in a *Christianity Today* article, "can give us a false sense of success because it can be learned by reading the right books and watching a couple of the latest TV shows. But thinking I can reach the youth of my community because I read a book on postmodernism and wear the latest clothes is a delusion."[12]

Ironically, by seeking to be culturally relevant, Christians may create a mindset of living in a realm away from the society around us. It denotes that we somehow exist over and above the culture in which we reside. H. Richard Niebuhr writes about many Christians who "emphasize the *opposition* between Christ and culture. Whatever may be the customs of the society in which the Christian lives, and whatever the human achievements it conserves, Christ is seen as opposed to them, so that he confronts [individuals] with the challenge of an 'either-or' decision."[13] This understanding causes us to try to relate with the world in a way that appears to be duplicitous to those outside of the Christian community. We are forced to feign interest and connection to a culture toward which we are ambivalent because we stand apart from it and somehow above it. Others rightly suspect the lack of authenticity accompanying such attempts at cultural relevance. Karl Vaters draws on a metaphor for this point:

> Chasing cultural relevance reminds me of an episode from the old TV sitcom *Third Rock from the Sun* in which the aliens tried to blend in with earth culture by doing what was popular. They watched only the highest-rated TV shows, wore the best-selling clothes, ate at the biggest chain restaurants, etc. They didn't do what they

12. Vaters, "Forget." Vaters appears to be referencing season 3, episode 22, of *Third Rock from the Sun*.

13. Niebuhr, *Christ and Culture*, 40, emphasis original.

enjoyed, only what was popular. As a result, they became bland and bored. By the end of the episode, they decided that being themselves was better than blending in.[14]

How can we be ourselves as the church? How do we live into the fullness of Christ's mission in the places we inhabit?

Being present is the new relevant. We are a genuine witness when we are faithfully present in our space and time. We earn the right to speak our voice on issues and in conversations by fully living into our context. We must be tuned into issues of injustice and the struggles of people who reside in our immediate context.

Our faith is best passed down through our experiences and stories. The era of distrust in which we are living embraces personal "truth" but denies universal truth. A cultural maxim today says that "your truth is right for you, but it may not be truth for others." Much of the time, Christian arguments against this relativistic claim are useless and come across as offensive. It is nearly impossible to argue that another person's truth is not truth for them. But rather than bemoaning postmodern relativism, we can use our response to this maxim as a great opportunity for the church! We can share with others our real, lived experiences through our changed lives. The stories of experiences are often appreciated by others, since they are narrated by us as known individuals and not imposed on others by a faceless institution. Our story is one articulation of the *kerygma*. Our stories of transformation can be a great witness. Story is the best evidence within a culture such as ours that values the real expression of personal truth. Our story, when accompanied by the Spirit's presence, can transform others. We do not need to rely on changing someone's mind about Jesus. God changes hearts toward Jesus.

The church is also a faithful witness to the world through our posture toward people who are hurting within an unjust society. Some have suggested that Luke 4 contains Jesus' mission statement. Jesus unrolls the scroll at the temple and quotes the prophet Isaiah: "The Spirit of the Lord is upon Me, because He anointed Me to preach the gospel to the poor. He has sent Me to proclaim release to

14. Vaters, "Forget."

the captives, and recovery of sight to the blind, to set free those who are oppressed, to proclaim the favorable year of the Lord."[15]

Jesus' use of this passage from Isaiah is a metaphor for the bondage of our souls to sin and the release of burden through resurrection in Christ. But the original, more literal understanding is essential for us to recover as well. We are a people committed to abolishing the injustices that are at our front door and beyond. The _kerygma_ that we proclaim is both the metaphorical and the literal interpretation of this command. The medium—the silver, iron, and lace of our craft—is our authentic presence within the community of those who truly suffer. This includes those who suffer from substandard schools, from skyrocketing housing prices, from hurtful immigration policies, from mass incarceration, from racial profiling, from drug abuse, and above all, from the absence of Jesus in their lives. Our radical love and hospitality speak into this medium, this context.

The giving—and even more so, the receiving—of hospitality can run counter to North American culture. Much of US history has been guided by the myth of individualism. By contrast, much of the Christian faith and mission is communal. This dynamic is a real opportunity for ministry. We are bombarded with messages that we should rely only on ourselves and look out for number one. But the picture we get of the church in the book of Acts is not an expression of self-reliance. According to the New Testament, the church is not a network of individually independent Christians. We struggle, instead, to operate as an inter-reliant church. Our modern context builds many barriers to interdependent community, and because of systemic inequities, many people can never achieve the ideal of responsible autonomy. Often our endeavors to engage those marginalized by the economy compounds this injustice. Well-meaning Christians try to live out the call to the poor by making people feel like they are charity projects. Acts 2 describes the first church, in which they "had everything in common" and "there were no needy persons among them."[16] These phrases point

15. Luke 4:18–19 NASB.
16. Acts 2:44; 4:34 NIV.

to community life together, not to charity. The church is called to be a revolutionary force within the constructs in which we live. As we train in the workshop of the Holy Spirit, our prayer is that we may be discipled out of the toxic ideology of self-sufficiency. We grow through the faithful presence of others on the margins. In his book *Reading the Bible with the Damned*, Bob Ekblad describes how his encounter with the Bible changed him once he read it with the marginalized. "I am convinced," he writes,

> that I learn more than I give during my encounters with fellow readers and the text. I have witnessed many men and women come to believe that God loves them in the midst of many obstacles and hardships. . . . [We] must seek out personal contact, always with an openness to listen in order to understand, recognizing our own tendency to distrust and judge. We must count the cost before naively trying to dismantle barriers that people on the margins have placed there to protect themselves from hurt and abuse.[17]

Isabel, a theology student, experienced deep poverty as she grew up among Hispanic gangs in California. The insecurity of her home environment produced "walls" (as she described them) when she was placed in unsafe situations. For the practicum portion of one of her theology classes, Isabel was expected to spend time with homeless teenagers. The task given to her as a volunteer was simple: she was asked to sit with others, make conversation, and try to fit in. But she found that she could not. Isabel was triggered emotionally by the perception of a lack of safety, and she shut herself off from the group. She was quiet and felt alone.

Unexpectedly to Isabel, the group of kids allowed her to be present even in her anxiety. Their acceptance eventually enabled Isabel to let her guard down. As she did so, Isabel began to interact with these young people, who carried a diversity of life stories. She fell in love with the community and its accepting nature. "I went there to volunteer but cannot believe how much they taught me,"

17. Ekblad, *Reading*, xiii, xvi.

she says. "I learned listening and acceptance in ways I knew before, but never really knew in my heart."

Collective Modes of Work

Some business trends can provide illumination for the craftwork in our medium—for living out the message of Jesus in our contexts. In 2014, *Harvard Business Review* chronicled how many businesses have moved toward the use of collective space for their mission. They examined Google, Facebook, Samsung, and others. The article begins this way: "In Silicon Valley the tight correlation between personal interactions, performance, and innovation is an article of faith, and innovators are building cathedrals reflecting this. Google's new campus is designed to maximize chance encounters." Yahoo's human resources chief is quoted as saying that "some of the best decisions and insights come from hallway and cafeteria discussions." There is a movement toward functioning with less hierarchy, more creativity, and collaborative space, looking for "that innovation you see when people collide."[18]

This is not only a movement of workspace; it taps into the basic nature of human flourishing. We work better with diverse others, who provide partnership and move us toward collective success. Paul describes church leadership as a connectivity of parts. In Ephesians 4, he writes about building up the church for ministry, addressing the nature of leadership for the church's growth, "for the equipping of the saints for the work of service, to the building up of the body of Christ; until we all attain to the unity of the faith."[19] Paul does not designate a particular individual within the church of Ephesus as the leader to accomplish this important task. Instead, he suggests that Jesus appoints a variety of people, "some as apostles, and some as prophets, and some as evangelists, and some as pastors and teachers."[20] Paul affirms a diversity of leader-

18. Waber et al., "Workspaces," 70. The final remark is by Scott Birnbaum, quoted within the Waber article.

19. Eph 4:12–13 NASB.

20. Eph 4:11 NASB.

ship that functions working as co-equals, with their appointments based upon roles rather than power.

Often, however, we are placed in ministry roles that can be dangerously autonomous. The role of a solitary senior pastor, for instance, without other people who also have authority and responsibility, can be daunting. The CEO style of church leadership reflects values of personal achievement orientation rather than the gospel. Frequently, this model minimizes biblical, role-based leadership models, the metaphor of the body of Christ, and the priesthood of all believers.[21] Some congregations rise and fall on the ability and stability of a single leader instead of the strength of the entire body.

Ronald Vallet vowed some very specific changes in his ministry should he return to pastoring. At age 73, he did just that, and one of the important changes he committed himself to was the way that his pastoral identity related to the laity of his congregation.

> The pastor will be seen by him/herself and the congregation primarily as a *theologian in residence*, rather than in the traditional roles of therapist/counselor (internal role) or the CEO/administrator (external role). Lay members of the church will be seen as full members of the church, not second-class citizens whose responsibility is limited to "temporal" matters. Together, pastor and people are entrusted with stewardship of the gospel at that time and place.[22]

In the New Testament, the people of the church are meant to share power. When a church cedes its authority to an individual, whose supposed responsibility it is to make the church all it needs to be, the structure strips the laity of their obligation and privilege for leadership and discipleship. It also places an ungodly amount of pressure on the individual pastor. Ministers can suffer from moral failings and burnout due to the high level of demands that they carry. Today's students are rightly wary of laboring in the workshop of their ministry craft without a team of journeymen, journeywomen, and masters. They are drawn to co-pastor models

---

21. Eph 4:11–13; 1 Cor 12; 1 Pet 2:9.
22. Vallet, *Stewards*, 165, emphasis original.

of ministry, nontraditional staffing ideas, and less hierarchical structures. Collective is the new successful.

We are deeply motivated by the modern ideal of self-reliance. For most of us, this focus on individual effort is an unexamined value that influences the way we think about life and church. As followers of Jesus, our discipleship means the denial of ourselves, which may include the denial of our right to privacy in areas of life such as our sexual ethics or our personal finances. It may include denying our right to purchase certain houses, cars, or other material goods. In like manner, might our discipleship also include denying our right to an educational model in which we are evaluated solely by our individual efforts?

Collective models of theological education are challenging ventures. In one instance, undergraduate students entered the second semester of a ministry preparation course already knowing one another well from their first semester together. The class had gone through many experiences that had stretched them while knitting them closer together. They were, nonetheless, about to have their enculturated educational norms challenged further in order to prepare them more fully for ministry. The professor wrote the students a letter, inviting them to step into a deeper example of Christian community, as modeled through the class experience. He offered to place all of the points earned in the class into one common semester score—that is, everyone would receive the same collective grade. He designed the challenge to teach them the need to rely on others, to ask for assistance, to identify the gifts of others, and to place one's valuable resources under the care of one another. The class agreed to the experiment. At the end of the semester, the greatest volume of student evaluative comments had to do with the communal grading system. The group agreed that this grading experiment was the element of the class they "learned from the most," though admittedly, it had also been very difficult for most of them to accept.

Though perhaps common grading is not preferable in your setting, other collaborative forms of theological education will help to create ministers who think collaboratively. *Christianity*

Today has a website dealing with issues of women in Christian leadership. In a 2012 article entitled "Collaborative Leadership," the author wrote that "one of the greatest gifts women bring to leadership within the church body is our social conditioning toward collaboration. The difference between 'Do it this way!' and 'What if we did it this way?' is subtle, but important. One of our greatest ways to influence the church is by modeling collaborative leadership, which is what all believers—men and women—are called to in the New Testament."[23]

Entrepreneurial Ministries

While some business models of organization may have led the church to incorporate unhelpful values, there is still a lot to be learned from industry movements, and particularly from entrepreneurial experiments. A business entrepreneur operates a business that has a greater level of financial risk. Many entrepreneurial businesses are startups. New companies are often needed in order to engage new products and services for their medium—their customer base. Their medium changes rapidly, so startups do things in new ways, entering into new markets and creating new products. According to *Business News Daily*, the valuable features of startups include engaging the founder's passion and personality; being agile, nimble, and authentic; incorporating an "anything is possible" mentality; and empowering employees and leaders to make their own contributions. These characteristics enable some of the most exciting technological developments on the business landscape.[24]

"Startup culture" is the application of this phenomenon to enterprises outside of business per se. Other fields have innovators that apply similar characteristics. Startup culture exists in medicine, for example, as some physicians attempt to meet patient needs outside of the standard healthcare industry. Startup culture exists in public school education, as individual teachers empower

23. Kent, "Collaborative Leadership."

24. Gausepohl, "Embracing." The word "nimble" in Gausepohl's piece is a quotation by Jon Schulz of Viant Technology.

do-it-yourself educational models and creative classroom design. Crowdsource fundraising invests in startups across the vocational spectrum. Startup culture challenges the lethargic practices of institutional maintenance. The church in North America is also learning a lot from embracing this culture of innovation.

Theological students today increasingly perceive a post-denominational environment. Millennials and Gen-Z folks seem less interested in perpetuating large, institutional church structures. The North American religious context may not be fully post-denominational, but a large number of theological students already view themselves that way. For decades, ministry students have been frustrated and fed up with the denominational struggles that have damaged collective Christian identity. Many emerging ministers do not mind theological or social policy differences, but they are bruised by differences navigated poorly. They perceive that the jobs available in ministry are merely maintaining institutional structures. They prefer entrepreneurial opportunities for innovative ministry.

Risk Is the New Safe

The institutional church needs a new set of craftspeople who understand their medium and are open to innovation, not only because of the decline in membership but because creativity is in the church's DNA. The church has a long history of renewal from innovators. The monks of the abbey of Cluny restored Benedictine forms of monasticism in the tenth century. St. Francis called the church back to simplicity within an increasingly materialistic Renaissance culture. The Protestant Reformers were *semper reformanda*, or always in the process of reforming. Catherine of Siena and Teresa of Ávila reinvigorated Catholic devotional practice, providing a spiritual undergirding for the Counter-Reformation. Philipp Spener renewed the call for the pietistic depth that he had seen in the lives of the Reformers but that had then been lost in the disputations of Scholasticism.

We are in another era of creativity and innovation. Tim So-erens is a ministry innovator in the Pacific Northwest. When asked about the relationship between his work and his denomination, he replied, "I am research-and-development for my denomination." Some denominations and churches are using their entrepreneurial ministers for research and learning. They now have "innovation offices" and have placed people in positions with titles such as Head of New Faith Expressions. While pastors in traditional parish settings may not understand the need for these new developments, many others know that churches must exhibit imagination and experimentation.

Business entrepreneurs are responsible for new growth in their companies. They dabble in new ideas and have a higher risk threshold than others in their field. These characteristics are necessary for the growth of the church in the coming decades.

In the first place, startups engage what Gausepohl, writing in *Business News Daily*, calls the founder's passion and personality. Christians affirm that we're made in God's image and likeness and that Christ embodies that image. Consequently, we "[fix] our eyes on Jesus, the pioneer and perfecter of faith."[25] God has built within each of us unique passions, giftings, and personality. We can learn to hear God's voice in and through these aspects of our lives. We find direction when we heed the particular distinctives that God has put within us—the passion and personality of our founder. Frederick Buechner famously describes this process of spiritual discernment. "By and large," he writes, "a good rule for finding out [your calling] is this: the kind of work God usually calls you to is the kind of work (a) that you need most to do and (b) that the world most needs to be done. . . . The place God calls you to is the place where your deep gladness and the world's deep hunger meet."[26]

Theo came to theological education from a blue-collar background, which resulted in a strong work ethic combined with academic curiosity. He engaged in ministry during his study and allowed his academic pursuits to shape his passions and

25. Heb 12:2 NIV.
26. Buechner, *Wishful Thinking*, 118–19.

perspectives. He tried interning in traditional pastoral roles, but when he did so, he experienced discord and a lack of fulfillment. During the summer, when a church position wasn't available and he needed employment to fund his education, Theo fell back on the tradesman skills that he had learned from his family. He enjoyed working with his hands and the camaraderie of a worksite. He experienced God's presence, for instance, when he worked with his youth group on new-carpet installation. Through these experiences, Theo's convictions drove him to look for ministry doing manual labor for the good of others. Today, Theo is a construction foreman on Habitat for Humanity worksites. He builds houses that are located not far from the classrooms that shaped his convictions. But it took him a few years of trying different ministry settings before he found the right fit for his passion.

Another attribute of entrepreneurship is the capacity to be agile, nimble, and authentic. These characteristics are foundational for ministry pioneers. Ministry is filled with trial and error, failure along with success. Being open to failure is a sign of good development, positive risk, and the leading of the Spirit. In a medieval workshop there was no expectation on day one that an apprentice would be 100 percent successful with his or her medium. Conversely, there was an expectation that the novice would commit developmental errors in order to make improvement—just like Theo, who tried different ministry settings before finding Habitat for Humanity. Agility, not effectiveness, is the answer to error. Being nimble, not competent, is the response to failure. Theo would have missed the ministry that fit his character and personality had he continued to pursue a more traditional church position. When our workshop Master is the Holy Spirit, our best posture is to be nimble. We hold our directions and convictions loosely, to be ready for the Spirit to move us.

There also needs to be an "anything is possible" mentality, with the Holy Spirit as our guide. The church has been engaging with the impossible from its inception. We serve a God who is not bound to present and future barriers. We have been given a prophetic vision for our world, as seen in the book of Revelation, which details the confluence of every tribe, tongue, and nation, and shows us that the unimaginable is part of God's future.[27] Such prophetic visions have inspired Christians across the centuries and all over the world. Martin Luther King Jr. was motivated by a prophetic imagination to challenge the world toward justice. He did so immediately after completing his formal theological education. The Spirit is similarly alive in ministry students across the world. There is unlimited potential for your impact in the kingdom of God.

Perhaps the most important attribute for ministry innovators from the list of startup characteristics is the empowerment of employees and leaders to make their own contributions. Your faculty are invested in your empowerment. Faculty are like the journeymen and women in that they will not be able to labor on their craft forever. Someday, faculty will leave the work of preparing ministry leaders. Like generations of leaders before us, we who are faculty and church leaders may be uncomfortable with some of the decisions and directions that will be taken by your generation. But we have a faithful Spirit who is teaching you well. Beyond the desire to see our own legacies continue, we trust you to make your mark. We want you to be entrepreneurial and to make lasting changes within the church. Now is the time for you to be innovative, to create, and to discern the Spirit. This is the path to making your mark on the world for the sake of the gospel.

Backstory Two—Philipp Spener's Pious Hopes for Theological Education

"The schools would, as they ought, really be recognized from the outward life of the students to be nurseries of the church for all estates and as workshops of the Holy Spirit."

—SPENER, *PIA DESIDERIA*[28]

27. Rev 7:9.
28. Spener, *Pia Desideria*, 103.

At the very beginning of what we now refer to as the modern era, Philipp Spener issued his bold challenge to the theological educators of his day. He indicted the reigning academic culture, which he believed was misguiding pastors-to-be in their training. Spener exposed the sad fact that faculty in these schools commended theological students for their intellectual aptitude and their scholastic achievement but failed to assist them in making practical application of their knowledge to the situations and injustices experienced by everyday people. Professors paid scant attention, he wrote, to the cultivation of students' virtue, or to the depth of their devotion to God, or to their cooperation with, and spiritual accountability to, fellow students.

The result was that theological students in Spener's day competitively demonstrated their scholarly ability over one another but couldn't inspire a congregation or instigate changes for the many ills facing society. Stated bluntly, theological academies in the late seventeenth century did not serve the needs of the church adequately.

Rather than merely complaining about the dangers of modern isolation and competition, however, Spener provided his readers with a compelling prescription for reform. He had very specific aspirations for how theological schools should operate. Schools that educate pastors and other ministry leaders should be, Spener wrote, "nurseries of the church for all estates."[29] That is, theological schools have the potential to be nurseries in the horticultural sense, places from which the seedlings of new spiritual ideas can sprout and flourish. Theological schools are not to be institutions dominated by negativism or cynical criticism of the church but rather places where enthusiasm and creative innovation are encouraged. A school of theology or seminary (a word that literally means seedbed) can be the location where faith is nurtured so that people grow up more and more into the likeness of Jesus.

In addition, Spener states that theological institutions (the "nurseries of the church") should train theological students to minister to people of "all estates"—every class and walk of life. The structure of Spener's society was based on distinct orders or

29. Spener, *Pia Desideria*, 103.

"estates," each of which designated a prescribed social reality. The idea of an estate did not refer only to economic class but extended as well to every social function, every profession, every trade, and every condition, such as being single or married, clergy or lay. In his book, Spener radicalizes this tiered conception of society. Instead of bolstering hierarchy, he declares that theological training should make stratified categories obsolete within the church. Theological schools, instead, are to invigorate the spiritual lives of every person.

Spener critiqued theological education's Enlightenment-era overemphasis on the pursuit of intellectual excellence alone to the detriment of piety and righteousness. Today's seminaries, born during the heyday of modernity, often glorify the path of academic autonomy critiqued by Spener. Rather than mimicking the modern idolatry of gaining ever-greater rational knowledge, Spener thought that theological schools should be "nurseries of the church" and "workshops of the Holy Spirit"—places where discipleship, mentoring, and teamwork are modeled for the betterment of the church.

Such workshops can be created today, even out of existing institutions. What is needed is for theological schools to become such workshops of the Holy Spirit. The church will only be as healthy as the institutions that train its leaders. Conversely, theological institutions will be relevant only to the degree that they speak to the needs of the church. This is the question: how does the church, through its academies, best "equip the saints for the work of ministry"?[30]

30. Eph 4:12.

3

Fellow Laborers

Working Together on the Craft of Ministry

In the workshop, craftspeople labored cooperatively, many apprentices working together along with journeymen and masters. Though each apprentice needed to learn certain necessary skills, medieval workshops didn't operate in a competitive mode. The workers in the shop combined their efforts in order to produce fine, high-quality crafts. They appreciated the synergy that was produced by the teaming together of many people in a single pursuit.

The mutual employment and attitudes of the laborers in the workshop demonstrated their *esprit de corps*. They took pride in their labor, even though their own names did not appear on the crafts they produced. Instead of an individual's name, the seal of the workshop went on the finished pieces, frequently the seal of the master craftsperson. Similarly, those of us in theological education are not ultimately doing our work for such-and-such university, for this-or-that seminary, for So-and-So's church, for any particular denomination, or even for ourselves. Rather, since we're in the workshop of the Spirit, it's the Trinitarian God who is the *bona fide* master to whom we're accountable and whose seal is placed on all our endeavors.

The sense of partnership in labor grew because of the relationships that developed between the various people in the workshop. In addition to working alongside each other, apprentices frequently lived together as a kind of family unit with the master and the master's family, since the master offered room and board as components of the contract with the apprentice. Today, many theological students find that an intentional living community assists them in their ministry training. While not everyone can avail themselves of such an option, it nevertheless rings true that whenever close relationships are developed between students and other students, and between faculty and students, a fellowship is created that greatly enhances study and learning.

This type of interactive learning environment recalls the reciprocity of the medieval workshop. Augmenting the teamwork that was evident in a workshop setting, the workshops themselves also banded together to form larger organizations called guilds. Guilds began to develop in twelfth-century towns across western Europe because of the economic benefits of cooperation. This distinctive feature of social and economic life helped to carry on many of the traditions that the masters of each craft observed in their lives and work.

Guilds had many purposes. They ensured the quality of the products of the various craftspeople and they also protected vulnerable, ordinary laborers from oppressive members of the feudal nobility, who often threatened to coerce them into serfdom. In addition to these important economic safeguards, guildhalls, the buildings where the guilds met, provided essential social functions. They became places where workers held religious celebrations (such as saints' feast days), engaged in charitable activities on behalf of destitute fellow townspeople, or simply enjoyed each other's company. Often, the guildhall was the cheapest spot in town to obtain a pint of beer![1]

Guilds had various names. The thirteenth-century clothiers of Cologne, Germany, for instance, called themselves *fratres* ("brothers") and collectively styled themselves as a *fraternitas*

1. Hollister, *Medieval Europe*, 58; Epstein, *Wage Labor*, 64.

("brotherhood"). These familial terms had been used for centuries to refer to religious fraternities or clubs. The appropriation of such relational concepts by medieval craftspeople demonstrates that they perceived direct connections among their skilled training, their spirituality, and their social lives.[2]

Interestingly, the rules of the cloth retailers' brotherhood in-cluded the provision that no member could bring another member to court, except for an egregious crime. They knew that they needed to support one another. Yet the guilds were not exclusionary, and it wasn't difficult to enter most trades. Anyone who learned the skills could become a member (called a *compaignon*, a compan-ion). The guilds were purposefully open to newcomers. Someone could become an apprentice and join the guild just by paying a fee, sometimes also providing food or wine for the other *compaignons*.

The collaboration that distinguished workshops and guilds is a helpful model for theological education today. Theological schools are places, for instance, where students can choose from many subject areas and types of expertise. Leadership in ministry is at its best when drawn from a wide range of sources, and those multiple sources are readily available through the auspices of a theological school. The leaders of the millennial and Gen Z church will need preparation from across many academic disciplines. They're entering into ministry in a world that is cross-culturally intelligent; consequently, they must be able to lead while address-ing issues of race, gender, power, and privilege. These new leaders will also need to be entrepreneurial. They may find themselves less frequently in traditional, congregation-based pastoral roles than their predecessors did. This emerging reality for how ministry is done will not leave behind longstanding models from local con-gregations that are part of institutional structures or denomina-tions, but it will require new approaches for a new future. Students must look across various fields of study and curricula to identify the resources required for their ministry preparation.

2. Epstein, *Wage Labor*, 86–90.

Cross-Disciplinary Preparation

A pastor or other ministry leader today needs to be a resident theologian, exegete, ethicist, cultural critic, small business CEO, marketer, finance manager, community organizer, coach, mediator, people developer, advocate, crisis intervener, counselor, public speaker, social worker, senior leader, and sometimes the church plumber. These many roles are demanding. For us to expect a two-to-four-year educational program to teach all of these skills is ludicrous.

You're entering a beautifully complicated vocation. Many people go into their first ministry positions and bemoan that "seminary didn't prepare me for this." But how could it? The old model of theological schools typically exposed students to the classic disciplines of Bible, church history, systematic theology, ethics, and various aspects of practical theology. But we now recognize that ministry training must be more expansive than merely these historic subjects of theological study. In order to be trained properly for the multiple roles listed above, you may need to read up on psychology, sociology, law, or business, or even take full-on courses of study in fields such as those and others. You may even need a certificate-level community college class in old-building maintenance! The complex job roles of a pastor today take significant investment in subject areas outside of schools of theology. We need cross-disciplinary education, which can be learned formally through coursework or more informally through apprenticeships alongside ministry practitioners. Similar to the education received by a general practitioner (family doctor), both theoretical coursework and clinical expertise, each in multiple areas, are essential in order to be proficient in the wide range of conditions that the leader of a congregation or ministry organization will diagnose.

In an ideal world, pre-ministerial students would take a large amount of undergraduate coursework, complete a full, graduate-level theological education course of study, train in a two-year apprenticeship, and participate in follow-up coaching. But this extensive period of preparation would take ten years! Since such a scenario is impossible for most students, an ongoing regimen of disciplined reading or taking courses in many fields of study will be crucial.

The liberal arts, such as philosophy, history, and literature, provide a strong grounding in written and oral communication—essential skills for ministerial leaders. Philosophy also develops critical thinking skills. A firm grasp of history helps pastors to recognize that all people have been formed by the contexts in which they have lived. Literature provides examples of good writing and sparks the imagination that is necessary for thoughtful preaching. Many times, the best sermons are seasoned by anecdotes or quotes from poets such as Emily Dickinson, Langston Hughes, or Denise Levertov, or classic works of fiction such as *A Good Man Is Hard to Find*, *Jonah's Gourd Vine*, *Jayber Crow*, *Silence*, *Things Fall Apart*, or *The Brothers Karamazov*—to name just a few. These literary works, along with film, theater, and other fine arts, can become exceptional theological sources for adult Christian education seminars or classes. Our minds expand when we read, see, or listen to these productions, and doing so helps us to think outside of our relatively small circle of experience.

In addition to a strong liberal arts background, ministry students also need to understand social justice theories, as found in the academic discipline of sociology. As noted in chapter 2, our engagement with the complicated problems of our day is critical to our proclamation of the *kerygma* in the contexts in which we live. Our complex times need leaders who are well versed in the nuances of negotiating issues of race, ethnicity, sexuality, and ability, to name just a few. Christian voices of color can serve as guides to dominant-culture churches (although it is important that congregations acknowledge the physical and emotional toll of this work and "affirm intentional times for [these guides] to take breaks . . . and have space to renew, recharge, and reconnect"[3]). All ministers must be proficient in this work. We need to develop these competencies through academic learning and then find specific ways to practice justice work in our communities.

3. McNeil, *Roadmap*, 113.

Becoming well-versed on issues of diversity and justice does not derive from uniform ideological approaches. One can learn through a variety of subdisciplines, such as social work, Christian reconciliation, or race theory. But whatever the scholarly approach, the fact remains that sociological understandings are critical to learn. There is a lot at stake. Many are counting on us to accomplish more than just doing no harm in communities that have experienced repeated injustices. There is amazing potential to support the lives of vulnerable people. The world expects the church to be qualified in helping others, and neighborhoods benefit greatly from activist congregations.

Knowledge of psychology is also essential. Our day-to-day ministry life consists of direct work with people and their emotional needs. Exposure to the elements of basic counseling will be covered in your practical theology or pastoral care classes. Situations of psychological need, however, are often more complex than our pastoral counseling capacities can handle. We must know when and how to engage psychology professionals; well-timed referrals can be lifesaving. In addition, crisis intervention is very valuable. Ministers with developed skills in the discipline of psychology are better prepared for precarious moments. Our confidence, built from competence, often disarms tense situations and puts others at ease. As ministers, we are more confident in navigating tenuous situations when we have had psychological training—and we also become very aware of our limitations and the need to refer.

It is valuable for us to do academic work in the area of positive psychology as well. For years, the psychology discipline focused on elements of the human personality that were maladjusted. Positive psychology is the study of human flourishing. The field examines elements of life that make people and communities blossom and find meaning. Our ministry practices will be strengthened by the study of these ideas because of the hopeful nature of the gospel.

We also benefit greatly from the acquisition of business skills. The mismanagement of money is sometimes a quick path to ministry disqualification. Financial negligence among Christian leaders is often unintentional and can be avoided with appropriate training in good business practices. We can easily attain basic accounting skills in classroom settings. The business field is also a good place for helpful resources around organizational change and leadership theory. Industrial and organizational leadership courses provide excellent models of strategic planning and conflict management. Similarly, study in the fields of education or the health sciences can be bridges to other sectors of society. Each of the areas of study that we have named, plus many others, can help pastors begin to grasp the aspects of the work that deal with institutions and systems. The way you navigate ministry change will have lasting effects on congregations and other organizations.

Many students engage disciplines outside of theology, like those described above, in order to receive greater preparation for their ministry. But some of your fellow students are already in other occupations and enter into formal theological education in order to make their lives in ministry more integrated with their full-time careers. In the past, the term *bivocational* was used to describe people in ministry who made a living from a source outside the church, primarily when ministry could not pay them sufficiently. Now, however, any person can be understood as bivocational when they combine ministry with another area of work or study.

Here are just two examples of bivocational ministry. Jenny Shaw Gebhart was a certified public accountant who derived great satisfaction from her work. Some years ago, she began doing volunteer church work on the side and gradually began to perceive a sense of call for ministry. But the call did not include giving up the CPA work that she loves. She went to seminary and got her master's degree in divinity while continuing her CPA work. After seminary, she served as associate pastor of a nondenominational church while remaining an accountant. She appreciated the fullness of her vocation. The roles were not bifurcated within her identity; they were a way to live into God's call on her life. In recent years, Jenny has entered once again into full-time CPA work. She uses her formation in theological education to frame the way she serves her clients and the community every day.

Similarly, Tymon Haskins combines various types of work into his ministry. A pillar of his community in South Seattle, Tymon runs remedial programs for a Seattle middle school while serving as an outreach pastor for his megachurch. He has always understood his work with vulnerable kids to be part of his ministry. Though formally situated within the education sector, Tymon serves in church-based ministry to Seattle's kids as well. He decided to get a seminary education to gain depth of insight and to undergird his work in the community.

The medieval workshop allowed apprentices to be trained in many varied elements of the craft. While folks in the workshop specialized in differing skills, every person learned from each other. The curricula of theological schools now recognize the advantages of this kind of apprenticeship. Theological schools know that ministry training isn't done only by studying the content of traditional theological subjects. They understand that broad exposure to ministry situations is one of the best learning practices, and they give credit to students for internships, field education, and contextual education in placement sites with pastors and other leaders. Through these experienced practitioners, students perceive how to be continual, lifelong learners.

Many of the wisest and longest-lasting pastors have found ways to use aspects of their day-to-day work as means to their continued growth. The pastoral vocation has an intrinsic component of study to it. The process of writing sermons, for instance, enables pastors to sharpen their learning on a weekly basis. And as Eugene Peterson wrote in several of his books, such as *Under the Unpredictable Plant, The Pastor,* and *Five Smooth Stones for Pastoral Work,* the ministerial vocation can continue to be life-giving over many, many years—if and when pastors take regular time to nurture their devotional lives through the discipline of *askesis.* Peterson defined *askesis* as the disciplined practice of reflection and communion with God through reading, writing, praying, and other spiritual practices.[4]

4. Peterson, *Under the Unpredictable,* 75.

Partnerships for Ministry

Cultivating collaboration in ministry, even during this time of your theological study, has the added benefit of providing a model of cooperation and mutual communication to use when you face polarizing debates. Such divisiveness seems to be taking place more and more frequently among Christians and in the broader society. Ministers and theologians have the opportunity during their training years to learn the craft of how to engage difficult or strident discourse in productive ways. Just because servants of God have political and theological differences doesn't mean that fellowship must end. The Holy Spirit, the Master Craftsperson, can teach the church to navigate these conversations generously.

We all encounter people who feel threatened by the diversity of perspectives that others have about the world and the Bible. Those with whom we engage theologically may oppose our positions aggressively or overconfidently. In such encounters, we can allow the Spirit to teach us a particular posture for our relationships with others, something known as *epistemic humility*, an attitude that we maintain throughout challenging conversations. While we stand firm in our knowledge of God's truth and our hope in the ultimate consummation of all things in Christ, epistemic humility means that we also recognize that we don't yet possess a fullness of understanding—that because of our finitude, we acknowledge the limits of our perceptions. At the present time, we "see in a mirror, dimly, but then we will see face to face."[5] Because we're aware of our human frailties, we're called to be gracious and honest when other committed Christians disagree with our positions and conclusions. Charity in contentious conversations isn't a sign of weakness or of compromising the truth; it's a skill in the path of negotiating difference.

Epistemic humility will allow us to use wording such as the following when we engage in conversations of theological difference.

---

5. 1 Cor 13:12.

- "I'm confident of the position I just laid out for you. However, I have to be intellectually honest and let you know that other positions exist. Those positions also use biblical evidence and church tradition. In fact, if a theological position has been controversial for centuries, it's probably because there have been differing biblical interpretations on the topic over a long period of time. Nevertheless, this is my faithful response to my understanding of God's call on this issue."

- "Since the Bible doesn't offer specific guidance on this topic, we need to apply other beliefs that we've discerned about God's character. Yet some Christians may stress different aspects of God's character and thereby come to different conclusions."

- "I'm not going to escalate this argument because I believe we both intend to please the Lord with our lives. I know that your heart wants to find the right path forward and I know that mine does also. I'm trying to be faithful to how I hear the call of God and I believe you are, as well."

In these statements, you can see distinctive elements that are charitable, intellectually honest, and leave room for differences—yet ultimately hold strongly to one's own point of view. Our ability to validate theological difference is extremely important in a society in which people increasingly interact only within their ideological bubbles, therefore engaging in dialogue that demonizes those with differing perspectives. We disarm volatile situations when we offer the benefit of the doubt and provide pathways for nonclosure, charitably assuming that the other person is also seeking the mind of Christ. We can use communication tools like these to defuse unnecessarily demeaning or conflictual situations while still staking out our theological ground. The ability to maintain a posture of epistemic humility doesn't indicate intellectual weakness. Just the opposite: having an attitude of epistemic humility is possible only when one has acquired an especially effective set of skills in argumentation and critical thinking—things you will develop through your theological education.

The vast differences within the Christian family of traditions can be seen as a gift to the church. Beginning in the nineteenth century and unprecedented in church history for its scale and rapidity, a wide range of denominations arose in North America. While it's true that there were doctrinal and ethical issues that had led to the Christian community's fragmentation—we're no strangers to that possibility in our own day—in general the various groups continued to live together in peace and genuine Christian charity as sisters and brothers, even while worshipping in different facilities and in forms that varied from one another. Writ large, the phenomenon was a witness that a plethora of Christian groups really could live alongside one another in (relative) harmony.

Here's an example of how these dynamics played out. In the center of my (Doug's) hometown of Springville, New York (population 4,000), is a major crossroads where Buffalo Street and Franklin Avenue meet. The four corners of the intersection manifested the values of the community when I was growing up. One corner held the village park. The other three corners were occupied by three different churches: Baptist, Methodist, and Presbyterian. They had all been built within just a few years of each other in the mid-nineteenth century. Everyone in town accepted that the members of all three congregations belonged to different, but still valid, expressions of Christian belief. That held true for members of other congregations that would establish themselves in Springville later—Catholics, Episcopalians, Lutherans, and Pentecostals (Assemblies of God). The spirit of Christian charity was still operating in town among the believers across all those denominations and after all those years.

Alexis de Tocqueville, a French historian who wrote a famous description of US society called *Democracy in America* after visiting the United States in 1830, observed that American Christianity flourished in this setting of religious diversity. Even the term *denomination*, which came to be used in the US to refer to any one of the many Christian groups in America, indicates (by the etymology of the word) that rather than viewing people from other sects as heretics or non-Christians, we view them as Christians who are "denominated" or "named" differently. People from other denominations are simply "Christians by another name."

When we learn to live and learn with a diverse group of Christians—something you may experience even *within* your theological school—we're under less pressure to have unanimity of belief while finding commonality of purpose in mission. Various types of Christian belief and practice can exist within a unified whole. While it's probable that we still prefer and strenuously argue for our own specific tradition's beliefs and practices, we are less insistent that our sect of the Christian family is closer to God. We trust that the craft of learning together to proclaim the *kerygma* will bring more and more people to the truth. A posture of hospitality and epistemic humility gives witness to the uniqueness of Jesus and welcomes those who are on the journey to find him.

Partnerships for Neighborhood Common Good

The most successful workshops always found processes by which to incorporate new workers easily. Onboarding people into the workforce provided the shop with fresh perspectives and different skill sets, allowing for breadth and innovation. Similarly, our cooperation with those who have positions different from ours can open up a world of possibilities for partnerships, not just in theological education but also in ministry settings. Many towns and cities, just like my hometown of Springville, have churches of various traditions at the same intersection, on the same street, or in the same neighborhood. To be honest, churches were often originally built next to each other out of competition, not for partnership. But today, the preponderance of churches is a great opportunity. Most congregations have independent budgets, staffs, programs, and services. Waning church attendance and finances may force us to work together. We can imagine partnerships with our faith neighbors through joint initiatives, through streamlining and sharing administrative costs, or by hosting vital neighborhood conversations. Our ability to get along with others has the potential to be a wonderful example of mutuality within American religious culture, which has more typically seen Christian segmentation than unity.

Paul's body-of-Christ metaphor from 1 Cor 12 can be applied beyond the congregational level. It's possible to see the church universal, even in its fragmented state, as the body of Christ. When we come together in harmony, we collectively witness Christ to the world. Some local churches are committed to a larger denomination while others are intentionally disconnected and nondenominational. Both denominationally connected and nondenominational congregations can benefit from a renewed version of ecumenism based less on theological positions or social issues and more on geography. Committing to neighborhoods and places of geographic proximity can be a bonding mission across congregations from various denominations. Ministerial alliances are a good start and often lead to a much more integrative and creative partnership among fellowships in a particular area.

Churches can engage creatively and also begin to move past traditional differences by working together for the proclamation of the good news of Jesus through common mission. We can recover the church's historic position of being a social convener, which is still alive in many non-White faith-based settings. This was especially evident during the middle third of the nineteenth century. A movement of religious revivalism, spearheaded by a preacher named Charles G. Finney, brought together Christians across denominations. The church was awakened to evangelism and the spiritual dynamics of the faith in spite of the dueling dogmas and sometimes fierce opposition among the various denominations. Significantly, the renewal of the heart provided pathways for social reform. Many of those who were revived spiritually went on to become abolitionists in the fight against slavery and engaged in multiple types of activism. The legacy of revivalism spread to the temperance movement, the women's rights movement, prison reform, educational reform, and many other causes.

Finney's combination of evangelism and social reform found a home at Oberlin College in Ohio. The theological education taught at Oberlin had direct fruit in effective preaching for conversion to Christ and advocacy for issues of social justice.[6]

Often, our theological education shapes the convictions that drive ministry for the rest of our lives. This was the case for Keary Kincannon when he was at Wesley Seminary. Keary began Rising Hope United Methodist Mission Church in Alexandria, Virginia, while a student. His desire was to plant a church whose ministry would be organized "around the pain in our community,"[7] the vulnerable people living along the Route 1 corridor of Fairfax County. A former addict, Keary believed in the power of the gospel to transform lives and culture. Rising Hope Mission has a strong commitment to the homeless in the area and found itself at the center of political attention in February 2017 when US Immigration and Customs Enforcement agents arrested seven men who were sheltered at the church on a cold night.[8]

Today, many churches lead coalitions of community businesses and schools to address issues of health, hunger, or literacy in neighborhoods. In Memphis, for example, urban local congregations have partnered for decades with community advocates from the nonprofit Methodist Le Bonheur Healthcare in order to facilitate better health among inner-city residents. The Center of Excellence in Faith and Health is the product of their collaboration, and part of its mission is to "bring together local faith community resources for education and training" of clergy and other faith leaders. It understands that "healing is more than treating specific symptoms. [The agency believes] in a holistic approach to [its] patients, attending to the mind, body, and spirit, which creates an important integration necessary to bring wholeness and quality of life." As a result, the Center offers a centralized hub for multiple churches and other faith-based groups to cooperate missionally in their own city—an "interfaith collaborative center of research, innovation, and training."[9]

6. Dayton and Strong, *Rediscovering*, 85–94.

7. Kincannon, "Home."

8. Hernández et al., "Federal Immigration."

9. Methodist Le Bonheur Healthcare, "Center."

The Center of Excellence in Faith and Health works closely with various partner agencies such as the Urban Child Institute (UCI). When the theologically trained director of the Center learned that one of the leading indicators of *physical wellness* was the presence of *increased literacy* among the young people of the community, she convinced multiple partner congregations and faith-based nonprofits to train volunteers to tutor elementary school children. Some local seminarians became involved, too. Since the volunteers weren't professional educators, the director established a relationship with a company that supplies a literacy app so that a volunteer only has to be available and present to read to the child. The result is that every year 800 children receive literacy training from volunteers at twelve afterschool sites throughout Memphis, most of which are church buildings. Some of these churches had been declining for years before the literacy program breathed new life into the congregations.

The director and her colleagues, most of whom had seminary degrees, discovered that their theologically informed commitments, combined with proficiency in sociological research and community organizing, provided a great melding of the abilities that were needed for leading-edge activism to deal with the injustices at hand. Theological education, when linked with real-life ministry, can be transformative for a community. And theological educators and students can be those people who assist in making collaborations possible.

Congregations can do much good on their own, of course, but they may become even more effective in their partnerships. Teaming with other organizations can also result in tremendous outreach. Those in partner institutions begin to see the relevance of the church because of how it declares hope for the world. When the COVID-19 pandemic swept through the United States in 2020–2021, Black churches were proactive in partnering with government agencies and local providers to provide health education and vaccine access to underserved communities. In one peer-reviewed journal article describing a COVID-19 prevention partnership between Mayo Clinic and local Black churches in Minnesota, the researchers write that "from its inception, the Black church has consistently served as a resilient source to mobilize community members for capacity building to reach groups that have been marginalized and oppressed at the most troubling of times—especially in the areas of health and social injustice."[10] As a result of their partnership, academic researchers came to see and describe the church in terms that reflect Jesus' proclaimed mission in Luke 4:18–19.

Some Christians find philosophical common ground for engaging their communities through community development programs such as the Christian Community Development Association, originally developed by John Perkins in Jackson, Mississippi, and the Asset-Based Community Development Institute. ABCD utilizes the assets of a community (businesses, schools, gifts of individuals, diversity, etc.) as a starting place for conversation and action, rather than using deficits (poverty, illiteracy, drug use, broken families, etc.). Initiatives have a much more positive spirit when community organizers ask how they can increase pride and hope in their communities instead of, "How can we get rid of all of the graffiti and make sure it won't come back?" An ABCD approach to community development creates a level playing field for participants and brings congregations into movements that already exist in their contexts. "In the Community Development context, the importance of social relationships is critical to mobilizing residents and is often a critical component for the success of a project or program. Social capital comprises the formal and informal institutions and organizations, networks, and ties that bind community members together."[11]

Lucy received ABCD training as a part of her theological education program. Each day was spent with classmates and the neighboring community. She watched a diverse group of community members come together across many socially dividing lines. They got to know each other, strategized, and shared heartfelt joys and concerns. Lucy received a great deal from this real-world

10. Brewer et al., "Emergency Preparedness," 2.

11. Haines, "Asset-Based," 48.

type of training. She immediately took the community development principles she learned into projects for some of her other
classes. She and two classmates, for example, began researching
the neighborhoods they drove through in the city, especially those
labeled as "troubled." They analyzed a particular neighborhood,
situated around a major intersection, that was receiving increasing amounts of negative news coverage. Lucy and her classmates
discovered that the neighborhood was located where three different school districts adjoined one another. They realized that the
neighborhood lacked identity because kids did not attend school
with their neighbors. Students who lived on adjacent blocks for
their entire lives might have gone to school miles apart. Lucy and
her friends found the closest church to that intersection and began
to get involved. They met many of the neighbors and began to take
steps to listen to them. After Lucy and her classmates graduated,
they moved into the neighborhood and found a vocational calling.

In all such interactions that you face, the Holy Spirit will guide
you. We suggest that you first place yourself in ministry situations
as a listener and a guest. It's good for you to suppress any notion of
needing to correct or even to contribute at all before you listen. The
first task in any new setting is learning, putting aside assumptions,
and asking questions. Getting involved in action will then help you
to understand the local context more deeply, which in turn will enable you to contribute meaningfully to the conversations.

Faith at Work Movement

Ministry as a vocation is far from the only outlet for a Christian's
calling. People in every profession have seen their work be their
"ministry." They feel a deep sense of God's presence within that
work. Especially since the time of the Protestant Reformation,
which emphasized the "priesthood of all believers," churches have
stressed that every Christian can be viewed as "religious"—not just
those ordained to the priesthood or to religious orders—and that
every job can be understood as a legitimate calling from God, unless that job harms yourself or others. Indeed, God is present in

every sector of society. Martin Luther and his fellow Reformers recognized that there is a paradox within the Christian faith: no one has special access to God. Because of Christ and the Spirit, no one needs a human mediator to come to the Father. Nevertheless, God calls some people for unique Christian service, to be leaders within the church.

Countless exceptional exponents of the Christian faith were not ordained clergy or even leaders in a church. Many Christians are working prophetically in sectors of society that do not have expressly religious missions. This was captured in the early days of the Faith at Work (FAW) movement. The FAW movement emerged in the 1980s as "a complex set of relatively independent developments," spearheaded by professionals and businesspeople who desired to integrate their work responsibilities with their personal faith. It has many forms and expressions, but at its core, it defends and promotes a "holistic lifestyle in which the whole self—body, mind, and soul—is important." This integration of faith and work does not just apply to the realm of the personal but is also concerned with the ethical and moral ramifications of how businesses and corporations function in the world.[12]

The FAW movement is currently being challenged to expand beyond white-collar and "marketplace" professions. Business for social good, education that transforms neighborhoods, blue-collar jobs, compassionate healthcare, stay-at-home parenting—all of these are arenas in which God is at work, calling us to integrate our spirituality with our day-to-day labor. The FAW movement is also being prompted to respond to individuals whose work is not intrinsically rewarding or affirming, those who do tedious, dangerous, or toilsome jobs for low pay, often enduring mistreatment or a lack of respect from employers. What does faith at work look like in situations of economic and occupational injustice and brokenness?[13]

12. All quoted material in this paragraph is drawn from Miller, *God at Work*, 6.

13. The material in this paragraph is drawn from Greg Forster, as featured in Bock and Forster, "Challenges."

Ministry Alone Is Dangerous

Whether or not you end up serving in professional church ministry or in whatever type of ministry you originally had in mind, your entire life has the potential to be "in ministry," no matter where and how it plays out. Many people have received theological educations but have made careers in things other than professional church work. Yes, you're investing a lot of time, money, and heart in your theological education. But this sacrifice will benefit you long after any student loans you may have are behind you. Your life as a devoted follower of Jesus will be better because of this enterprise. You will make better decisions on ecclesial matters, you will be more reflective when faced with challenges, and you will forever see ministry as more than a job.

But over and above your years in formal theological education, your long-term, sustainable life in the Spirit is our greatest desire. Ministry that is bifurcated from the rest of life is dangerous. It is not an ideal expression of our call to have times and places when we put on our pastor hat and other times and places when we take it off. Life in the Spirit is the place from which ministry flows; life in ministry is not the axis on which your life in the Spirit spins.

The improper use of power can be a negative factor in every profession. In professional ministry, that temptation is especially cruel. The ways in which clergy abuse power compromise their call. When pastors hurt people, they can crush someone's hope that a clergyperson will become a mediating presence who partners with God.

We negotiate power when speaking the Word of God to others. We engage in relational power dynamics when discerning spirits with others.[14] We adjudicate power as a conduit of healing for others. We are careful with power when guiding others in a life-changing relationship with Jesus. These aspects of ministry are close to our hearts, since it is due to our reception of life-changing power that we are students in the workshop of the Holy Spirit in

14. 1 Cor 12:10.

the first place. All of us must tread reverently and lightly around these manifestations of power.

Henri Nouwen was an Anglican priest who left his position as a Harvard professor to live and work at L'Arche, a home for adults with developmental disabilities. Transitioning from a position of power to a "small, hidden life" with people who had no interest in his accomplishments was transformative for Nouwen. He wrote *In the Name of Jesus*, a book of reflections on Christian leadership, soon after moving to L'Arche, and it offers us a view of what Christian leadership looks like from a place of hiddenness and community. He identifies three primary temptations for Christian leaders: to be relevant, to be popular, and to be powerful. The temptation to power, Nouwen writes, is most potent when intimacy feels like a threat, because it "offers an easy substitute for the hard task of love. It seems easier to be God than to love God, easier to control people than to love people, easier to own life than to love life."[15] True spiritual power, Nouwen discovered, is corporate, and it is harnessed when a leader chooses a path of downward mobility and submission to a community. This looks like a willingness to listen and be led, to be vulnerable and trusting, and to engage in confession and forgiveness.

We should handle with great care the souls and the work that God offers us for ministry. Our reverence for the work and the sober acknowledgment of our fragility ought to lead us continually to prayer and honesty. Students can easily put on a front for ministry. There is a misplaced logic to it: "If I am perceived as a spiritual leader, then I must have my act together. But I know that I do not have all areas of my life in order, so I will (consciously or unconsciously) hide my areas of weakness." We are incredibly vulnerable to lies and temptation through this deception. Over a long period of time, we can come to believe anything we tell ourselves. We can start to believe that, somehow, we are spiritually, relationally, intellectually, or emotionally superior. We can take liberties with the advice we give to others and speak with broader authority than the gospel gives us. We can begin to believe that our particular

15. Nouwen, *In the Name*, 59.

calling means that the church's expected standards and relational boundaries do not apply to us.

You are hopefully growing in holiness. You may "graduate" out of some of the behavioral problems of the present. However, some struggles are lodged in the deeper places of our hearts. These trials include insecure motivations, thirst for power, and unforgiveness. The most profound challenges are not "conquering" issues: they are "management" issues. Our goal should be to keep them from killing us and our ministry. We struggle our whole life long, they force humility through humiliation, and we ultimately find the grace of Jesus through them.

We should all be grateful that God does not call us to a brand of perfection for Christian service. Instead, we journey with the Holy Spirit, who grows us along the way and gives us outlets for staying connected in the midst of our struggles. Our ministry is dependent not on our spiritual temperature but on the Spirit's empowerment of our journey toward holiness.

Honesty in ministry is paramount. However, our honesty needs another person to receive it. Elsewhere in James the writer admonishes us to "confess your sins to one another, and pray for one another so that you may be healed."[16] Yet it is vital to choose the right people and safe places for trustworthy sharing. To be most honest is not always to be most helpful. Transparent authenticity is dangerous without wisdom.

In all these situations, we need the accountability of others. Every theological tradition provides opportunities for such accountability. In the Catholic and Orthodox traditions, confession became formalized through the sacrament of penance, in which the believer confesses to a priest. Other traditions have other means. In the Lutheran and Calvinist (Reformed) traditions, it is customary to include a prayer of confession in every worship service, and certainly before the reception of the sacrament of the Lord's Supper. Pietism, the tradition of Spener, developed the practice of small-group accountability for spiritual growth and confession. The Moravian sect called these groups "band meetings." John

16. Jas 5:16 NASB.

Wesley, the founder of Methodism, was greatly influenced by the Moravians. Wesley appropriated the idea of band meetings as a place for sanctified growth through regular confession. He also established "class meetings," which were somewhat less intrusive but still stressed accountable discipleship.

Power and Identity

It is important to realize how closely power is tied to identity. Medieval guilds were open to newcomers, but they were not all-inclusive. They were "patriarchal, hierarchical, and elitist institutions that excluded most men and women from membership."[17] Although there were some women who achieved independent guild status, most guilds had formal restrictions against admitting women; in some cases, women were even barred from working in incorporated trades.[18] In the same way, many churches and seminaries have historically been places where a person's ability to hold, exercise, or share in power is determined by their gender, sexual, racial, or ethnic identity. Tara Beth Leach, the former senior pastor of First Church of the Nazarene in Pasadena, California, writes about how difficult it can be for a Christian woman to internalize her God-given giftedness as genuine and not inferior to others.[19] Her prayer, and the theme of her book, is that Christian women may be *emboldened* and empowered to flourish as leaders. That same prayer can be extended to anybody with an identity that has led to their being sidelined, overlooked, or actively discriminated against despite their giftings, particularly in Christian spaces. For these individuals, theological training will ideally provide an emboldening community in which to develop the confidence to speak and move with the authority to which God is calling them. This requires a combination of both confidence and humility, as well as a community in which power is truly shared and each voice has weight.

17. Crowston, "Women," 43.
18. Crowston, "Women," 43.
19. Leach, *Emboldened*, 37.

Repairing broken systems and confronting power imbalances requires working together, but not every individual is called to the same kind of work; "it will look different in various places, depending on the context, with particular work for different people and communities to do."[20] When individuals with privileged identities recognize the power they effortlessly embody and make intentional decisions to shift the balance, and when there is space for open and honest dialogue about issues of power, identity, and intersectionality, such conditions dramatically increase the likelihood of a learning community becoming a space where a diversity of believers will thrive and have their voices heard.

Heather became a divinity student after spending decades in complementarian churches, which taught that pastoral leadership roles were biblically limited to men. One of the things that initially startled her in seminary was that her own voice and contributions carried equal weight with the male voices in the room. Additionally, in her classes, students and faculty freely named and discussed issues of privilege, justice, and identity. Although this had been true in her secular education, this was the first time Heather had experienced the same dynamics in a Christian space. Not only did she feel seen and validated as a full person, but she also gained confidence in her own giftings, insights, and vocational call. She learned that walking in humility was not incompatible with speaking with directness and authority, and that she did not have to apologize, compensate for, or underplay either her feminine identity or her abilities. As she became more assertive in her church and sought out a position of leadership there, her seminary community listened to and encouraged her, naming and affirming her potential. They emboldened her to lead.

Teamwork in Theological Study

At Heather's school, all entering first-year seminarians devote themselves to a five-day, retreat-based course that takes place just

---

20. McNeil, *Becoming Brave*, 188.

prior to the regular fall term, held at a conference center on Puget Sound within sight of the Olympic Mountains on scenic Whidbey Island, Washington. This course, known as "Christian Formation through Discipleship," introduces students to the craft of theological study and a number of historic Christian disciplines, such as the daily office (including Holy Communion), singing worship songs as a communal spiritual practice, *lectio divina*, journaling, sharing testimonies, the prayer of examen, "class meetings" (accountable small groups), and the Moravian love feast. Students read and study about the tradition of each discipline and then practice it as a community. (This course is followed by an urban experience in the students' second year, called "Christian Formation through Mission.") Seminarians continue to meet in discipleship groups during the rest of the school year, sometimes with professors or staff participating.

This course-retreat, along with the ongoing formation that takes place throughout the year in weekly small groups, creates an environment of mutual trust and support that percolates into seminary classes. When students find themselves in heated discussions regarding hot-button ethical issues, for example, instead of reacting with disdain and condescension toward classmates, they remember that they worshipped with those colleagues or they recollect what the other persons shared about their backgrounds, all of which helps them to empathize with the others' perspectives. This common experience allows sharp argument and vigorous disagreement to flourish while maintaining deep fellowship in the Spirit.

Community

Drawing from the significance of the weekly small-group experience in the lives of seminarians, the larger Christian university in which this theological school is embedded[21] launched an initiative that provides the same small-group experience for all 700 freshman undergraduate students as part of their introductory theology

21. Disclosure: it's the school where Doug has served for fourteen years.

course on Christian faith. This comprehensive spiritual formation venture originated from the pedagogical conviction of theology faculty not only to teach about Christian faith but also to provide a winsome experience in Christian formation, along with a desire to address the pressing need for spiritual development among young adults through mentoring and peer relationships. Such mentoring operationalizes the biblical mandate of 2 Tim 2:2, in which Paul encourages his pastoral apprentice this way: "What you have heard from me through *many witnesses* entrust to *faithful people* who will be able to *teach others* as well."[22] Building on this model, theologically educated faculty and staff train seminarians ("many witnesses"), who have already participated in their own accountability groups, to train and mentor upper-class undergraduate student leaders ("faithful people"), who then lead small groups of college freshmen ("teach others").

The small groups embody a practice in Christian formation that exposes students to Christian community, facilitates growth in awareness, and engenders love for self, neighbor, and God. To accomplish these purposes, participants gather weekly under the leadership of a trained student leader to ask and answer a traditional formative question: "How goes it with your soul?"

Begun in the eighteenth century, John Wesley's original "class meetings" brought people together, as he put it, "to inquire how their souls prosper; to advise, reprove, comfort, or exhort."[23] The groups created a sacred space for people who were seeking God at any level of faith to grow together in community.

The program is the university's adapted version of these historical groups. The one-hour-per-week meetings provide an opportunity for a student-led, authentic witness to the reconciling work of Jesus Christ. The small groups are not Bible studies or prayer meetings, nor do they have any formal academic requirements, such as research papers or tests. Rather, the sole content is for students to speak to one another about the state of one's soul—the deepest self, the self before God that lies beneath surface experiences and

22. 2 Tim 2:2, emphasis added.
23. Wesley, *John Wesley*, 178.

emotions. Undergraduate students in the Christian Faith course participate in the cocurricular small groups as a learning opportunity. They learn about spiritual formation in class and then put into practice what they're learning in their weekly groups.

A typical freshman's reflection speaks to the value of the experience: "In relation to my spiritual growth, the group helped me to reflect on how I . . . want to please God. My group leader was very good at saying she would pray for us. When people offer to pray for me, it has this way of helping me feel like I'm not alone. I felt very supported and then also offered to pray for others in hopes that they'd feel the same way I did." The greatest impact of the experience may even be with the upper-class undergraduate student leaders. Each undergraduate leader is mentored by a seminarian, who leads the undergraduate to explore his or her own faith development. As one undergraduate leader wrote: "Spending time with members of my college community and reflecting on important things like my relationship with God is very life giving. Following Jesus is a lifelong journey and it means giving my life to Jesus. My small group is a way for me to give my life to Jesus. I absolutely love leading these small groups. I feel so filled and blessed by them and it makes me feel I have a place where I am . . . making a difference on campus. I feel like this is a calling from God."

While the particularities of this university and seminary may not work in every setting, mentorship and collaboration for spiritual growth and discipleship can be adapted in many ways and places. How are you being discipled? How are you discipling others? What might you do to develop a mentoring relationship? How can your community provide regular opportunities for honest spiritual reflection and accountability?

Teaming together with others may not always seem like the easiest way to live out your vocation or accomplish your purpose. Medieval workshops provide us with a helpful model of collaboration and shared power, but they were not perfect. They inevitably dealt with personality clashes between group members, negotiated sharp differences of opinion on how best to complete projects, and were not immune from the surrounding culture's prejudices and power imbalances. In the same way, Christian communities are composed of imperfect people and will never live up to the ideal we write about and long for, at least not on this side of eternity. Dietrich Bonhoeffer, who led an underground seminary in Germany during the Nazi regime, wrote that Christian community "is not an ideal which we must realize; it is rather a reality created by God in Christ in which we may participate."[24] That participation may be challenging at times, and it will look different from another person's participation depending on your identity or background. It may involve letting go of power in order to share it, or it might mean stepping into the authority to which God is calling you. It will involve conflict and disillusionment. We persevere in community when we trust that our imperfect collaboration is inhabited and empowered by the triune God, who has provided us with the gift of each other in order to form and train us into competent craftspeople whose work bears the seal of our Master.

Backstory Three—The Modern Enlightenment Misstep in Theological Education

It's no accident that theological schools, and institutions of higher education in North America more generally, have emphasized an orientation of personal accomplishment rather than more collaborative approaches to education. Unlike the teamwork and relative anonymity of craftspeople laboring together in a workshop, colleges and universities are better known for their stress on individualized success in a meritocracy based on high achievement. Where did this academic individualism come from?

Universities, as we know them now, originated during the same time that the craft workshop and guild system was becoming dominant, in the late medieval period. And similar to workshops, universities were made up of masters (professors) and apprentices (students). Each of the earliest higher education institutions, founded at Bologna, Paris, Oxford, and Cambridge, referred to

24. Bonhoeffer, *Life Together*, 30.

itself as a *universitas*—a guild-like community of teachers and scholars. From the thirteenth through the mid-sixteenth centuries, these academic communities all connected themselves closely with the Christian church, and the study of divinity became one of the scholarly pillars of a university education, standing beside law, medicine, and the liberal arts in status.

Following the devastation of the Thirty Years' War and other religious conflicts of the sixteenth and seventeenth centuries, however, academicians influenced by Enlightenment thought started to challenge the concept that scholarly study should be closely tied to the church.[25] When Philipp Spener wrote his Pietist book on theological education in 1675,[26] many of his peers disputed the older idea of an ecclesially oriented education. The medieval concept of church-based education was falling away, just as the medieval concept of craft workshops was transitioning to the capitalist economic system of industrial factories. When Spener called upon theological schools to become places where students would work together jointly with their professors in a spiritual workshop, he was summoning theologians to return to the type of educational system that had previously been common. In Spener's view, theology ("study of God") is best engaged by believing Christians under the guidance of the church, and it should be the centering discipline for all education.

The newer model of university education found its apex at the University of Berlin, instigated by scholars like Wilhelm von Humboldt and the theologian Friedrich Schleiermacher. Prussian King Friedrich Wilhelm III founded the University of Berlin in 1810 to be a research university independent of all influences, especially from the church. (Ironically, however, the institution continued to be strongly influenced by Prussian politics.) Regarded as the world's premier university for the natural sciences in the nineteenth and early twentieth centuries, the "Humboldtian" model of secular higher education became the example for all subsequent Western universities, including in the US, particularly for schools

25. González, *History*, 87–109.

26. Spener, *Pia Desideria*.

such as Johns Hopkins University (1876) and the University of Chicago (1890). The latter school played a major role in the development of the discipline of "religion" (as opposed to "theology") as the phenomenological and supposedly objective study of humanity's striving after the divine as a compartmentalized academic field within American universities.

The Humboldtian educational model derived from the Enlightenment idea of the self-determining individual, enabling students to become autonomous individuals by developing their own reasoning through academic freedom. Teaching and research centered on the work of the individual scholar. People could become competent teachers, merchants, or businesspeople if they received schooling based on unbiased knowledge and analysis, independent from religious influences. Obtaining an objective view of history from studying original documents was seen as an attainable goal.

In practice, the study of theology moved from the center of the university to a minor corner, if it remained at all. In attempting to provide an intellectual place for religion on par with other Enlightenment disciplines, Humboldt and Schleiermacher actually narrowed religion, displacing it from its role as a God-centered lens of revelation through which one interprets the whole.

These changes in educational method occurred more than a century after Spener's life. Nonetheless, by Spener's day, Enlightenment principles of individualism and the claims of objectivity were already marginalizing the claims of theology—a harbinger of a future that Spener correctly foresaw. Modern theological education, even at many religiously based universities, follows the Berlin model of independent, autonomous research. There is irony in separating the study of religion from the church, the place where religion is actually practiced. Imagine, for example, studying medicine apart from any clinical medical practice! Theology works best when it is done collaboratively and in dialogue with where it is embodied and practiced: the church.

4

Journeymen and Women

Sustaining the Day-to-Day Responsibilities of Education and Ministry

SKILLED ARTISANS WHO SUCCESSFULLY completed their apprenticeships in a trade or craft became journeymen or journeywomen. This status meant that they were considered competent and authorized to work in their fields. Because they were skilled, they often commanded substantial wages. Journeymen and women earned their licenses through education, supervised experience, and examination. Guidelines were put in place to promote responsible tradespeople who would be held accountable for what they produced, protecting their particular trades and the general public from work of poor quality once such men and women were established as proficient. As qualified tradespeople, they could eventually become masters themselves and run their own businesses, though not all did so.

The name *journeyman* preserved the original characteristic of their status: they did day work and were paid per workday (the word *journée* in French means "day"). In actual practice, however, most masters did not employ journeymen on a day-by-day basis but preferred contracts that had terms of employment for many months, sometimes as long as a year or two.

Journeymen and Women

The journeyman was not yet a master. Though skilled, journeymen and women still had much knowledge to acquire and expertise to demonstrate in order to qualify for those titles. Interestingly, in English, the word *journey* now refers to continuous travel, which fits well with our contention that theological study is an ongoing, lifelong adventure. The earlier use of the word to describe a daily occupation fits as well, for the journey of ministry is both open-ended and day-to-day. The role of the journeyman or woman is comparable to the "long obedience in the same direction"[1] of ministry—the necessary cultivation of wisdom and virtues over time. This is the daily, and sometimes tedious, labor of becoming an expert in the craft—of improving one's skills and thereby moving from competence to excellence.

Tools are essential for doing excellent craftwork, and they must be good tools. Poorly made tools don't last over time. Masters of some crafts passed down sets of quality tools to apprentices at the end of their service, just as the apprentices were entering into their work as journeymen or women. Historical records show, for instance, that every master blacksmith in Genoa, Italy, during the twelfth and thirteenth centuries gave such a set to her or his apprentices. The basic tools for these *ferrari* (an Italian surname meaning "blacksmith"[2]) were a hammer, an anvil, and a pair of tongs. Other trades practiced a similar custom of providing high-caliber tools.[3]

What are the tools needed for successful theological study—the practices that will help you to receive the most out of your educational experience? Even more importantly, what practices will sustain ministry for years to come?

In a craft workshop, one will frequently find framing tools and shaping tools. Framing tools are often large instruments that help the craftsperson to form the object being created: devices like a loom or an anvil or a potter's wheel. For pastors and theologians, such framing tools include biblical study, the systematic

---

1. See Peterson, *Long Obedience*, esp. 12, 17; Peterson's title comes from Nietzsche, *Beyond*, sec. 188.

2. Ferrari Lake Forest, "What Does Ferrari Mean?"

3. Epstein, *Wage Labor*, 69.

or constructive wrestling with theological ideas, the acquisition of knowledge about the tradition of the church, the practice of ethical reasoning, the study of the sociology of religion, and so forth. These large academic and vocational tools frame one's ministry into an overall form that hopefully resembles the *kerygma* of the gospel message.

A workshop also contains shaping tools—implements that help craftspeople to do the fine work of finishing an object. These are precision instruments. Shaping tools include equipment like a shuttle or a jigger or a chisel. For pastors and theologians, our shaping tools are the spiritual practices that shape our ministry in the church, the fine tools that allow someone to do the precise honing of caring for and supporting people's lives with God's love. Unlike what happens in an actual workshop, however, these precision instruments of spiritual practice have the potential to shape not only the completed craft item of ministry but also the craftsperson him- or herself. As we practice the shaping tools of spiritual disciplines, we are formed into the image of our Creator and Master.

The life of the journeyman is comparable to the first years of your theological study. This season involves the daily and sometimes grueling work of becoming adept at using your framing tools, the skills of your vocation, even as you also practice the shaping disciplines of the Spirit, which integrate head, heart, and hands. What are the particular shaping tools that will sustain your ministry for years to come? Which habits, disciplines, and convictions are essential to the life of a minister? Can these qualities be cultivated during your theological education years even if they come from somewhere other than the curriculum in a classroom?

Tools for the Work

The very first Christians, after responding to the Holy Spirit's outpouring at Pentecost, "devoted themselves to the apostles' teaching and fellowship, to the breaking of bread and the prayers." They also

practiced communal worship and fasting.[4] These shaping tools—
Scripture meditation, Christian fellowship, communal worship,
the Lord's Supper, prayer, and fasting—have been central to Christian spiritual practice from the earliest days of the church to the
present. Other practices, arising from particular contexts or cultures throughout Christian history, have also become significant
avenues to connection with God, and most theological traditions
endorse a set of practices that shape their communities of faith.

The Desert Fathers and Mothers of the fourth and fifth centuries discovered that silence and solitude were a "furnace" in which
powerful personal transformation could take place.[5] Eastern
Orthodox Christians use material images, such as icons, as invi-
tations or windows that open up to the divine, transforming presence of God.[6] The Reformers of the sixteenth century developed
hymnody into a popular communal spiritual practice that has
endured in Protestant churches. In John Calvin's words, singing
hymns together "both gives dignity and grace to sacred actions,
and has a very powerful tendency to stir up the mind to true zeal
and ardor in prayer."[7] For the Puritans, spiritual journaling became
an important devotional discipline, a tool for self-examination and
a "means of grace" that "could provide clues to God's plan for the
soul" and help the writer grow in holiness.[8] Women, in particular, used their journals to "contemplate and demonstrate spiritual
leadership," expressing themselves in a way that would be "otherwise inhibited by conventional behavioral codes and restrictive
practices."[9] In Black churches, the call-and-response format of a
typical sermon is a corporate shaping tool, involving listeners in

---

4. Acts 2:42; 13:2–3; 14:23.

5. Nouwen, *Way*, 20.

6. Irvin and Sunquist, *History*, 363–64.

7. John Calvin, quoted in Hilbrands, "Psalms," 69; see also Baum et al.,
Ioannis Calvini, Institutio III.20.32.

8. Hambrick-Stowe, *Practice*, 186.

9. Lindman, "Beyond," 153.

the act of proclamation and thus becoming "an expression of the holy God working through the preacher and the community."[10]

These examples are just a few of the many practices that Christians around the world have found to be helpful tools for the spiritual journey. There is no magic in these particular disciplines, and they are not the only ways we connect to God. Spiritual formation also could include practices less institutional to the church that grip our souls: things like dance, music, hip-hop, visual arts, adventure and physical risk, engagement with nature, and other embodied activities. In the classic movie *Chariots of Fire,* Eric Liddell struggles to explain his decision to train for the 1924 Olympics rather than to focus exclusively on his call to the mission field. "I believe that God made me for a purpose, for China," he tells his sister. "But he also made me fast, and when I run, I feel his pleasure."[11] Activities that make us come alive and "feel God's pleasure" are often ways in which we are uniquely created to connect with God.

John Wesley, whose example and writings shaped the Methodist denominations, the Church of the Nazarene, and other holiness groups, as well as many charismatic and Pentecostal traditions, was particularly concerned with the heart of religion and the practices that form us. He taught that God provided us with particular tools, or "outward signs, words, or actions," that convey grace to our souls.[12] God does not need us to practice these tools in order to meet and transform us, and we can never force God's intervention or attention through our actions. Nevertheless, God consistently uses these "means of grace" to renew our souls and shape us into the image of Christ, and our practice of them sustains our faith. Wesley's list of these "means of grace" is based on the practices we observe the early church performing in the book of Acts: searching the Scriptures, prayer, fasting, receiving the Lord's Supper, worship, Christian community, and acts of compassion. In this chapter, we will focus on these particular means of grace as the shaping tools that sustain a life of faith and service,

10. Crawford, *Hum,* 16.

11. Hudson, *Chariots,* 59:11.

12. Wesley, "Means," 187.

although we could just as easily use categories of spiritual practices from other Christian traditions.

Searching the Scriptures

Christians throughout history have relied on Scripture as a source of guidance and transformation. For Wesley, the Bible was one of the initial means of grace, not because it provides us with a "cold, objective standard" to live up to, but because of its "unique ability to bring men and women into an encounter with Almighty God."[13] He called the practice of reading the Bible for personal transformation "searching the Scripture"—prayerful and reflective reading in which we open ourselves to the voice of God speaking to us through the text.

The role of the Bible in the life of the believer has been written about extensively. Resources for Bible study include everything from simplistic formulas to exhaustive inquiries meant to keep us pushing deeper into God's Word. Studying the Scripture will nurture us. However, prescribed methods are often counterproductive. They make us feel guilty when we lack inspiration or discipline. "Searching the Scripture" is not the same as reading it for information, nor is it the legalism of a daily discipline. It is necessary to acquire a comfort with Scripture by reading and "mastering" its content through theological studies. We grow personally from our public performances of it and our deep study of it for theological and ministerial work. But our relationship with it does not end there. Ruth Hailey Barton writes that we need a "way of being with Scripture that allows God to initiate with us (beyond all the ways we seek to control such things) and also creates space for us to respond fully."[14] As we assume this posture of receptivity, we find that our practice of searching the Scriptures can more truly be described as the living and active Word of God searching and penetrating *us*.[15]

13. Harper, *Way*, 29.

14. Barton, *Sacred Rhythms*, 54.

15. Heb 4:12.

Lectio divina ("divine reading" in Latin) is a method of allowing the Scriptures to search us that has been practiced for centuries. It "involves a delicate balance of silence and word"[16] as we read and reread a short passage of Scripture in a way that helps us to listen and respond to God's Spirit. In her book on spiritual practices, Marjorie Thompson describes this process using the images of both a dance (with God as the initiating partner) and a cow chewing its cud (we repeatedly chew and digest God's word "until it brings forth new life and energy that can be shared with others").[17] *Lectio divina* begins with a period of silence (*silencio*) in which we rest in God's presence and ready our hearts to hear the Spirit speak. This is followed by four readings of our chosen passage. In the first (*lectio*), we listen for a particular word or phrase that resonates with us. During the second reading (*meditatio*), we reflect on how this word interacts with our own life, desires, and longings. As we hear the passage a third time (*oratio*), we identify the response toward which God is prompting us. The final reading (*contemplatio*) is an invitation simply to rest in God's loving presence, "receptive to whatever God desires to do with us."[18] We then return to the business of our day, resolved "to carry [what we have heard] with us and live it out (*incarnatio*) in our daily life."[19]

Allowing the Scriptures to search us constitutes a truly formative, lifelong process. I (Jess) felt a call to ministry and began my college theological education shortly after an experience of conversion, having only read seven books of the Bible. The academic rigor of biblical study confounded me. I quickly realized that I was behind my peers who had attended teenage youth groups or catechetical programs of various kinds. Out of desperation, I committed that I would read the Bible every day during the summer after my freshman year. I was driven by the fear of not being able to handle the course of study in front of me. In three months, I read the entire Bible from cover to cover with a pastor

16. Barton, *Sacred Rhythms*, 55.
17. Thompson, *Soul Feast*, 24–25.
18. Thompson, *Soul Feast*, 24.
19. Barton, *Sacred Rhythms*, 58.

and a small group. It was an incredibly formative summer for two reasons. First, I was encountering God's Word, which allowed me to scrutinize my life in valuable ways as an emerging adult. Second, the discipline of that summer stayed with me as I resumed my theological study. My fear and desperation had been replaced with rigor and curiosity. God used that hunger through the rest of my theological studies, and I excelled in ways I had never imagined.

Prayer

In his classic book on spiritual formation, Richard Foster writes that "of all the Spiritual Disciplines prayer is the most central because it ushers us into perpetual communion with the Father," bringing us "into the deepest and highest work of the human spirit."[20] One thread that unites the stories of Christian saints through the centuries is their common reliance on prayer as an essential and sustaining practice. The Christian faith is a life lived in relationship with God through Jesus Christ, and prayer is central to maintaining that relationship. John Wesley believed that prayer was "the gift of God to humankind to facilitate and enrich the relationship."[21] Through prayer, we have a real, lived, mystical experience with the divine that sustains our faith beyond any practices, theology, routine, or tradition.

Remember the story of Seth from chapter 1, and how it was prayer that got him through the storms of his theological education? The assertion that prayer is a sustaining power through your education and first years of ministry may seem like a trite and simplistic sentiment. But remember that the means of grace are not doctrines or good ideas. They create spaces in which God meets us and transforms us.

Prayer comes naturally to some, while others need to train the mind, heart, and spirit. As we practice the shaping tool of prayer, we are invited to listen to and learn from Christians

20. Foster, *Celebration*, 33.
21. Harper, *Way*, 19.

throughout history who left us details of their own journeys of learning to pray. The diversity of their experiences demonstrates that although prayer may be a common thread among them, there are as many ways to approach the throne of God as there are individuals.

St. Teresa of Ávila was a sixteenth-century Carmelite nun and doctor of the church.[22] Her autobiography gives us a glimpse into her prayer journey, which ranged from "friendly intercourse and frequent solitary conversation" with God[23] to mystical, ecstatic visions. She described the work of spiritual formation as "setting out to make a garden for [the] Lord's pleasure, on most unfruitful soil which abounds in weeds."[24] Although it is God's work to pull the weeds and replace them with good plants, it is our work to water the garden, and we do that through prayer. In the beginning, our efforts in prayer will feel like drawing water from a deep well with a bucket. It will be heavy labor, and "the intellect will grow tired."[25] But then, as we persevere, our soul enters a second phase of prayer. It begins to work in concert with God, and the process takes less labor than it did before. It is as though we have the help of a pulley, and our "intellect now works very gently and draws up a great deal more water."[26] The third stage of our prayer journey is likened to drawing water from a stream or spring rather than from a well: prayer feels less like hard work and we experience the "pleasure, sweetness, and delight" of God's presence.[27] Finally, we reach the final stage, or the "fourth water." This is when God's grace rains freely down on us

---

22. "Doctor of the church" is a title given by the Roman Catholic Church to saints who made significant contributions to theology or doctrine. As of this book's publication, only thirty-six individuals throughout history have been named doctors of the church, and St. Teresa is one of only four women to have received this honor. See "Chronological List."

23. Teresa of Ávila, *Life*, 63.

24. Teresa of Ávila, *Life*, 79.

25. Teresa of Ávila, *Life*, 79.

26. Teresa of Ávila, *Life*, 99.

27. Teresa of Ávila, *Life*, 112.

and we experience pure joy: "the soul realizes that it is enjoying some good thing that contains all good things together."[28]

St. Teresa spent more time describing the first stage of the prayer journey than any other, because she understood the effort and discouragement we experience as we begin to train our minds and our hearts toward God. Prayer practices that involve our bodies can help us remain centered and focused. These could be as simple as kneeling and opening our hands, or they could involve taking a hike outside and allowing creation to connect us with the Creator. Walking a labyrinth or praying the Stations of the Cross are embodied experiences that can guide and direct us. Sometimes it is helpful to pray words that countless others have used to petition and praise God, such as the Psalms or the *Book of Common Prayer*. Christians from the Eastern Orthodox tradition teach that mindfully repeating the simple Jesus prayer ("Lord Jesus Christ, Son of God, have mercy on me, a sinner"), will turn our minds and hearts toward God and "result in [our] being with him constantly whether alone or with other people."[29]

Recent popularized mindfulness and meditation movements have allowed us to learn the patterns of our thinking and brain activity. They are often valuable tools for teaching us how to pray. We learn techniques to identify anxiety as it is happening, recognize fear, and slow our minds. When we are capable of mindfully engaging our thoughts and anxieties, our spirits find the space to rest in God's peace. In those prayerful spaces, one's spirit connects with God's Spirit.

My (Jess's) own experiences with prayer have evolved. They unfold in seasons. As I discipline myself to engage silence, it becomes easier to access deeper places in prayer. I go through prosperous seasons of motivation for the inner work of the spirit, and then I go through seasons of difficulty. Prayer will change over time, sometimes because our own efforts and rhythms change, and

---

28. Teresa of Ávila, *Life*, 122.

29. Theophan the Recluse, quoted in Chariton and Ware, *Art of Prayer*, 90–91.

sometimes because God chooses to communicate in a way different from what we're accustomed to.

St. Teresa of Calcutta (Mother Teresa), known to the world for her compassionate work with the poor and the dying in Calcutta, "ran on prayer," as one close observer remarked: "drained, exhausted and empty after a schedule which would have daunted much younger people, she would retire to the chapel and emerge after an interval manifestly revitalized, 'filled' and ready to continue God's work."[30] For Mother Teresa, much of her prayer did not involve words; instead, it was in the silence that she met God. "I always begin my prayer in silence," she wrote "for it is in the silence of the heart that God speaks. God is the friend of silence—we need to listen to God because it's not what we say but what He says to us and through us that matters."[31]

Mother Teresa had spent enough time in the furnace of transformation no longer to need words to communicate with God. This does not mean that she experienced constant intimacy with God. Even as Mother Teresa faithfully trusted and served God and they listened to each other, she struggled through long periods of silence and seeming abandonment. "The place of God in my soul is blank," she wrote to a spiritual advisor. "When the pain of longing is so great . . . then it is that I feel He does not want me—He is not there. . . . Sometimes I just hear my own heart cry out 'My God' and nothing else comes. The torture and pain I can't explain."[32] Even when God seems distant, however, prayer remains a means of grace, as we reach out to God and trust that we are seen and transformed. In her garden metaphor, St. Teresa of Ávila acknowledged that sometimes, for reasons known only to God, the well we draw water from is dry—but that even during these droughts God "preserves the flowers without water, and in this way he makes our virtues grow."[33]

Renita Weems, a prominent Bible scholar and minister, describes what it is like when prayer and spiritual disciplines seem to

30. Spink, *Mother Teresa*, 180.

31. Teresa of Calcutta, *Mother Teresa*, 7.

32. Mother Teresa, *Come Be My Light*, 2.

33. Teresa of Ávila, *Life*, 79.

go dry. "Call it a prayer block, a spiritual lull, the wilderness experience, the dark night of the soul," she writes in her book *Listening for God*. "But eventually and invariably we all find ourselves suddenly wrenched into an inner abyss."[34] She initially blamed her seeming disconnect with God on having given too much energy to relationships or the busyness of family or work, but then she realized that these disorienting periods were a regular part of her spiritual journey: "The occasional periods of inspiration and awe seem always to be followed by longer periods of spiritual ennui."[35] Her movements in and out of these seasons seemed like a spiritual failure. However, she learned that maybe her judgments of "failure" and "success" needed to change. Eventually she decided to surrender to the pattern and "trust the winter months of faith, when it's difficult to remember why one even bothered to believe."[36] Deprived of her accustomed ways of communicating, Weems learned to listen patiently in the silence and the emptiness. She came to perceive God "in new, amusing, laughable, glorious ways"[37] through her ordinary life as a spouse, parent, and neighbor. Weems reminds us that God's deep and formative work in us often takes place during the periods in which we're least aware of it, when prayer feels like nothing more than showing up for duty.[38] God's means of grace are not dependent on our own spiritual temperature or the season in which we find ourselves.

Worship and the Lord's Supper

Richard Foster introduces worship as our "response to the overtures of love from the heart of the Father."[39] To worship is "to know, to feel, to experience the resurrected Christ in the midst of the

34. Weems, *Listening for God*, 33.

35. Weems, *Listening for God*, 33.

36. Weems, *Listening for God*, 36.

37. Weems, *Listening for God*, 16.

38. Weems, *Listening for God*, 36.

39. Foster, *Celebration*, 158.

gathered community."[40] As a means of grace, worship is both a way in which we are served and loved and fed by God, as God's Spirit touches our own, and our human response to God's divine initiative; it is something we *do*. "Worship ushers us into the presence of the living God," writes Thompson, "and demands the attention, receptivity, and response of our whole being."[41]

Worship is primarily a corporate means of grace; it is something we practice together. The word *liturgy*, which describes the words and actions we perform together in worship, comes from the Greek *leitourgia*, which refers to the work or service of the people.[42] As we worship in community, we proclaim the greatness of the triune God, we offer ourselves as living sacrifices,[43] and we retell the story of what God has done in the past, reenacting it in the present, particularly through the act of taking Communion. "Thus these very acts of Christ again become present with all their power to save," writes James White, a liturgical historian. "What Christ has done in the past is again given to the worshiper to experience and appropriate in the present."[44]

John Wesley taught that "it is the duty of every Christian to receive the Lord's Supper as often as he can," both because Christ commanded it, and because "the benefits of doing it are so great."[45] The bread and wine are nourishing not just for our bodies, but also for our souls, even when we can't directly sense any benefit.[46] "The Mass is the spiritual food which sustains me," wrote Mother Teresa about her work in Calcutta, "without which I could not get through one single day or hour in my life."[47]

Breaking bread together is also a communal discipline; it connects us with one another and with God's world. Henri

40. Foster, *Celebration*, 158.
41. Thompson, *Soul Feast*, 54.
42. Thompson, *Soul Feast*, 53.
43. Rom 12:1.
44. White, *Introduction*, 25.
45. Wesley, *John Wesley*, 335.
46. Wesley, *John Wesley*, 343.
47. Mother Teresa, *My Life*, 96.

Nouwen claims that "the breaking of the bread stands at the center of the Christian community."[48] We remember that we, too, are broken, and that Jesus' broken body is offered to us. "When two, three, ten, a hundred, or a thousand people eat the same bread and drink from the same cup, and so become united with the broken and poured-out life of Christ," Nouwen continues, "they discover that their own lives are part of that one life and thus recognize each other as brothers and sisters."[49] Communion, then, prepares and strengthens us to love each other well and engage in works of mercy and compassion in the world.

Although worship is a gift of the Holy Spirit and not something we can achieve, there are avenues we can walk that guide us into a posture of worship. According to Richard Foster, the first avenue into worship is to "still all humanly initiated activity" and be quiet before God. This is not meant to be an attitude that we reserve for formal worship services, but a lifestyle that permeates our daily lives.[50] One of the most powerful means to this kind of lifestyle is to practice the Sabbath.

A medieval midrash (classic rabbinic interpretation of Scripture) claimed that creation was completed not on the sixth day when human beings were made, but on the seventh day with God's gift of *menuha*, or rest—a reality that reflects the "rest, tranquility, serenity and peace of God."[51] In resting on the seventh day, God delighted in God's own creation and invited humanity to do the same. To practice the Sabbath is to participate in God's experience of delight in the goodness of what's around us, to notice it and relax in it. We take a break from our work, ministry, and school-related deadlines and anxiety, not because we've earned it, but because we accept it as a gift. Sabbath is an invitation to let go of what presses in on us and trust that God holds us and our families and the world safe and provides for us. When we participate in this gift of rest, we are better able to notice and delight in the beauty

48. Nouwen et al., *Compassion*, 110.
49. Nouwen et al., *Compassion*, 112.
50. Foster, *Celebration*, 166.
51. Wirzba, *Living*, 33.

and joy that are woven throughout creation and our own lives, to be still before God in a posture of worship and prayer.

Practicing the Sabbath isn't easy for busy theological students and those involved in vocational ministry. Sundays are often not days of rest, and it will take creativity and intentionality to carve out and guard substantial spaces of grace and rest in our lives. It will definitely necessitate the occasional "no"! When Heather, a mother of three who was heavily involved in her church, began seminary, she decided to practice the Sabbath intentionally as a spiritual discipline. She quickly found that this was a practice that impacted her entire week. It required her to plan ahead and change how she structured time and responsibilities on other days of the week. And it challenged her to give up control in areas of her life in which she was tempted toward perfectionism: to settle for turning in a paper that was "good enough," to let go of responsibilities that were unnecessary for herself or for anybody else, and to push back against overcommitment. What surprised Heather was how freeing this practice became, and how much she came to anticipate and cherish Sunday afternoons and evenings as a time when she was present to her husband, her children, and the beauties and delights of the world around her. Sabbath observance became a gift that centered and renewed Heather each week, opening up a wider doorway of opportunity for her to enter into worship and to connect with God and others.

Fasting

Next to prayer, fasting is the spiritual discipline most frequently mentioned in Scripture. Fasting was a normal part of Jewish life, commanded by God in the Hebrew Scriptures, instructed in the New Testament, and practiced by Jesus' followers. We see it practiced in the text as a means of supplication in dire circumstances; in preparation for a mission (Moses on Mount Sinai; Jesus in the desert; Barnabas and Paul before their first journey); in the context of discernment; and as a normal part of a rhythm of confession and worship.[52] However, although many people understand the clear scriptural witness, they have not been taught how to engage in this complex practice.

There is a fine line between seeking God through fasting and trying to manipulate God into performing magic in your life. Fasting should not be practiced as a silver bullet for self-improvement or as a means to weight loss. It is not meant to be a test of endurance or a gauge of spiritual commitment. Thompson stresses that fasting is not "a discipline through which *I* gain greater control over my life, but one through which *God* gains access to redirect and heal me in body, mind, and spirit."[53] Fasting is a tool that viscerally reminds us of our total dependence on God, revealing "our excessive attachments and the assumptions that lie behind them."[54] As we voluntarily deprive ourselves of material nourishment, we are reminded of the ways in which "we put the material world ahead of its spiritual Source"[55] and we return to God's sustaining power. In this way, fasting becomes an opportunity to feast on what God alone can provide for us.[56]

Like prayer and searching the Scriptures, fasting is a long-term learning experience. It cannot be grasped unless it is practiced in seasons over years of discipleship. If you are a beginner, it is essential to come into fasting with a plan, listening to the experiences of others, and learning to walk before you run. You should not simply jump in and go as long as you can without eating. You may want to begin by fasting for a particular reason over a short time. It is often helpful to find a discipline of engagement while doing your discipline of denial. You may try replacing your mealtimes with a particular practice or act of compassion. Think creatively by engaging something you enjoy or spending intentional time devoted to a cause about which you care. It is also very helpful

---

52. Esth 4; Jonah 3; Exod 34:28; Matt 4:2; Acts 13–14; Matt 6:16; Luke 18:12.

53. Thompson, *Soul Feast*, 77, emphasis original.

54. Thompson, *Soul Feast*, 71.

55. Thompson, *Soul Feast*, 71.

56. Foster, *Celebration*, 55.

to fast in community. Choosing a spiritual confidant or accountability partner will not break Jesus' injunction in Matthew 6 to fast
in secret.[57] Jesus was addressing those who may use fasting as a
public way to show their righteousness.

If you have struggled with an eating disorder in the past,
fasting from food is not a healthy or wise choice. It can become a
trigger toward relapse and a stumbling block to recovery. Despite
your best intentions, there is a high risk that your brain will distort
the discipline to bring harm. Some other health conditions, such
as diabetes, also preclude fasting from food. Instead of restrict-
ing food, think of fasting in terms of temporary abstinence from
something you depend on for your emotional well-being. Perhaps
you could fast from social media, the Internet, or your usual means
of unwinding, replacing the time you would spend on these activities with a tool of engagement with God.

Naomi learned about fasting in her college's spiritual formation class. She felt drawn to it long after the class ended. She began
fasting two nonconsecutive meals each week. During the time she
normally spent eating, she instead wrote letters to estranged family
members, read books on world poverty, and devised direct-action
justice campaigns for her church. She used fasting as a discernment technique and also found deeper ways for it to be a shaping
tool on the spiritual journey.

Christian Community

It may seem unnecessary to find a church while you study. Schools
with a church heritage are often good at creating community
climates. Such colleges and universities are designed to provide
everything to meet your needs and typically offer regular religious
services. This is precisely the reason to find a church during theological study. In congregations you will find people living lives that
are not daily immersed in the study of God like yours will be. They
are living their theology without the privilege of PhD-level guides.

57. Matt 6:16–18.

They make their decisions and encounter God through life's everyday, off-campus dilemmas. Church community can provide you with a necessary perspective: not everything about the enterprise to which you are committed is about you. Furthermore, it can be profitable to your development to find a church community that offers you respite and the opportunity for corporate worship while you navigate the disorientation that frequently accompanies theological study.

Similarly, it is imperative that you have a community in place as you leave your theological institution. You will need a small group or an entire congregation you are committed to for the transition after graduation. You will need guidance that comes from a source external to your school, a Christian community that can provide you with direction, celebration, and accountability. L. Gregory Jones and Susan Pendleton Jones write that the three most important concerns to students transitioning into ministry from theological education are leadership, pastoral identity, and friendship.[58] Since theological schools are often good at providing friendship and Christian community, the skills to sustain those kinds of relationships outside of an institutional structure may be underdeveloped if your classmates and professors have been your sole Christian community.

Too many students believe that their perspectives, callings, or questions are simply out of bounds for the typical church. But when a student takes such a position, they are unwittingly saying that they must be the only person in the history of Christendom to think certain thoughts or to question certain positions. The church and the academy have often been in partnership as checks and balances to one another. Sometimes this dynamic has been seen in the historic movements regarding doctrine and mission. Other times, it has been seen in the life of a student who marvels at the community gathered for Eucharist even as she writes a paper deconstructing its historical significance. The church gives students already embedded in study and theory a community in which they can observe and embody what they are learning through incarnate participation.

58. Jones and Jones, "Leadership," 18.

The shaping tool of Christian fellowship and community goes beyond church attendance and participation. It also encompasses practices as quotidian as walks, coffee breaks, or meals together with friends and family. In *Life Together*, Dietrich Bonhoeffer—writing, you may remember, from his experience leading an underground seminary and intentional Christian community in Nazi Germany—details the necessary spiritual practices that hold a community together, such as prayer, Scripture reading, and the Lord's Supper. But he also emphasizes the importance of simply sharing food together on a regular basis and the delight that often results from it. "The fellowship of the table has a festive quality," he writes. "Our life is not only travail and labor, it is also refreshment and joy in the goodness of God. . . . Through our daily meals [God] is calling us to rejoice, to keep holiday in the midst of our working day."[59] Incorporating time for leisurely, shared meals into our weekly rhythm can be a sustaining and life-giving tool for us.

Acts of Compassion

As we discuss all of these precision shaping tools, it is essential to remember that they are not ends in themselves, but means. They help us to be shaped and formed into wholeness for the sake of others.[60] Just as Jesus' life, death, and resurrection brought about our redemption, our participation in the life of Christ will be oriented toward the redemption of our neighbor and of the world, and Jesus' self-giving love will "become the goal, purpose, and style of our lives,"[61] expressed in concrete acts of compassion that meet both spiritual and physical needs. Howard Thurman, the influential twentieth-century theologian and civil rights leader, wrote that "whatever we learn . . . in the discipline of silence, in meditation and prayer, bears rich, ripe fruit in preparing the way for love."[62]

59. Bonhoeffer, *Life Together*, 68.
60. Mulholland, *Invitation*.
61. Chilcote, *Recapturing*, 101.
62. Thurman, *Inward Journey*, 188.

In his book *Compassion*, Henri Nouwen eloquently describes the intersection where spiritual disciplines and the concrete love of neighbor meet:

> Acts [of compassion] do not stand beside the moments of prayer and worship but are themselves such moments. . . . Precisely when we live in an ongoing conversation with Christ and allow the Spirit to guide our lives, we will recognize Christ in the poor, the oppressed, and the down-trodden, and will hear his cry and respond to it wherever he is revealed. Thus, action and prayer are two aspects of the same discipline.[63]

John Wesley summarized his philosophy of service and action in three simple rules: "do no harm," "do good," and remain constantly "attending upon all the ordinances of God."[64] Although these are simple principles, effectively living them out can be messy and complicated. They have a strong social dimension and require us to think about how our own lifestyle or embodied privilege negatively affects those who do not share it. They call us to concrete acts of helping the poor and marginalized as well as to advocacy and action to repair broken systems. They call us to solidarity with the oppressed.

It is important to distinguish between acts of compassion and frantic activism. Compassionate service is difficult and often feels futile. We don't always see results or experience the joy of justice accomplished. When we shoulder the weight of the world's brokenness and judge our effectiveness by the visible results of our efforts, we are tempted toward activism and can become exhausted and embittered. Henri Nouwen reminds us that acts of compassion are not our tools but God's, and that we simply participate in what God has already done and is doing:

> In Christ, human suffering and pain have already been accepted and suffered; in him our broken humanity has been reconciled and led into the intimacy of the relationship within the Trinity. Our action, therefore, must be

63. Nouwen et al., *Compassion*, 119.
64. Wesley, *Methodist Societies*, 69–71.

understood as a discipline by which we make visible what
has already been accomplished. Such action is based on
the faith that we walk on solid ground even when we are
surrounded by chaos, confusion, violence and hatred.[65]

We are only able to sustain such faith through the grace of God,
which shapes and strengthens us as we practice the precision tools
of spiritual disciplines.

Renowned nineteenth-century novelist Fyodor Dostoyevsky
gives a profound example in *The Brothers Karamazov* of how acts of
compassion can themselves become tools to shape, strengthen, and
sustain our ministry. He tells of a wealthy woman who comes to a
monk because she suffers from a lack of faith. The monk explains
how she can gain assurance of her faith and the immortality of her
soul: "By the experience of active love," he says.

> Strive to love your neighbor actively and indefatigably.
> In as far as you advance in love you will grow surer of
> the reality of God and of the immortality of your soul. If
> you attain to perfect self-forgetfulness in the love of your
> neighbor, then you will believe without doubt, and no
> doubt can possibly enter your soul. This has been tried.
> This is certain.[66]

It is strange to call works of mercy, loving your neighbor,
or service to the poor "tools." Perhaps at this point our metaphor
breaks down. The activity and discipline of service is spiritually
formative. It is not done for that motive per se, but it does have
long-lasting and important ramifications on our life in ministry.

Keisha came to her theological studies as an adult with children. She soaked up every opportunity her education afforded her.
Her school sponsored an immersion trip to a small town on the
Mexican coast over spring break one year. During the trip, students
lived with families, often sleeping in the only bed in the house and
eating food prepared by people living in poverty. Keisha attended
the trips for three successive years, taking two of her daughters

---

65. Nouwen et al., *Compassion*, 121.

66. Dostoyevsky, *Brothers Karamazov*, 63.

with her. Keisha recalls the trips as formative for her studies, but a bigger impact was seen in the lives of her young children. In the years since, her whole family has built its life in service to North Portland, Oregon. Keisha wisely saw the potential of the type of experience she had in Mexico to build into her children the active love that Dostoyevsky suggests is essential to our faith.

Competence in Process

Transitioning from ministry training into the journeyman stage of development is exciting. You are both ready and in process at the same time. Ray S. Anderson expresses this evolution as moving "from a theology of ministry to a ministry of theology."[67] Your competency has grown through your theological education and will be tested within ministry settings. This is very good. Our growth is lifelong and our dependence upon God is the strength we bring with us. Anderson tells a story of realizing the limits of his theological education in ministry. "The seminary," he says, "gave me a very good rear-view mirror! Instead, I was caught in the headlights, so to speak, by the luminous faces of those who turned toward me seeking the person of God, not merely mental constructs about him. Theology becomes a curse when our concepts of God conceal the being of God."[68] The shaping tools of spiritual practices can keep us from this collision. We must resist the urge to make a mental construct of God instead of fostering our real, lived experience together.

Your greatest sense of confidence comes from competence. But there is great assurance from the experiential knowledge that God has called you for a reason, will be with you in the challenges, and knows the paths before you. Within this framework your theological education shines. You will be able to make ministry out of the convictions and knowledge you are working so hard for during these preparation years. We transform our training into

67. Anderson, "Making," 27.
68. Anderson, "Making," 29.

ministry when we engage our work with both the framing tools of a well-informed theology for the decisions ahead of us and the shaping tools of practices that help us maintain our awareness of God's presence. This combination reassures us of our status as children of God equipped for the journey we are on.

Supervised Experience

There are aspects of our lives in which it's important to be competent from the very beginning. Doing it right the first time is essential for paying our taxes or driving on the freeway. Doing the work of ministry, however, is not one of those areas. Formal programs of supervised ministry, field placement, or contextual education vary widely among theological schools. The best programs last longer than one term, teach contextual skills, and involve prearranged relationships with local ministers who understand the important role of challenging and supporting neophyte ministers in their initial experiences.

Supervised learning is essential because you will not be competent in your first ministry experiences. You will inevitably grow through your mistakes, and those mistakes will sometimes hurt people. It's crucial to have mentors and coaches who can bring a broader perspective to your experience as those dynamics unfold.

Some students find themselves overzealous in the early years of ministry. They trade the process of leading within community for the instant gratification of correcting or being prophetic with their perceived truths. Others struggle to find their voices and abdicate important opportunities out of fear. Humility and forgiveness are partners in the supervised ministry years. They are key aspects of the curriculum in the workshop of the Holy Spirit. Those virtues are your teachers *and* your lessons. A life of ministry is a crucified life. You will be wrong and will wrong other people on a regular basis. You are wise to practice confession and accept the awkward and humbling gift of forgiveness from the very people God has asked you to serve.

But you will also be delighted as you see specific growth in your work. I (Jess) was a terrible public speaker in my theological education years. I am indebted to a small and aging church I attended during college and seminary. The pastor and congregation graciously endured my sermons that ranged from too long to too short, obnoxiously self-righteous to completely fearful of the task, overintellectualized to pathetically shallow. Although I was genuine and authentic in every sermon, my preaching was a window into my sporadic and inconsistent development. My church community suffered through many sermons until I learned the secret of engaging my particular creative process and finding my truest voice. I reaped enormous dividends from their patient endurance. I was able to get a dream job as a college chaplain, a role that depended upon my ability to speak in public. I owe that church an incredible debt as I look back on the often judgmental messages that they heard me preach at them.

I (Doug) also gained immeasurably from my field education church placement. I made many mistakes and I frequently felt that I was in over my head. But the congregants and the supervising pastor were patient and encouraging. I grew in confidence and competence.

Supervised ministry, whether formal or informal, is at its best when it places you on the edge of your comfort zone. You will learn the care of the Holy Spirit by taking positive risks with the confidence of supervision backing you up. Life in the workshop of the Holy Spirit is a practice and repractice of stepping out in faith. You may deliberately decide to do supervised ministry in contexts beyond your familiarity. You can choose experiences that get you into relationships with those outside of your theological background, your racial and cultural groups, or your social class.

One program brought students into a Black charismatic church led by an awe-inspiring minister with a strong personality. He could quote Scripture to support every decision he made and every aspect of his church's life and operation. He did not hesitate to ask students to defend the biblical and theological frameworks underlying their own church perspectives. Most students experienced significant theological dissonance. Many aspects of the service, theology, and supervisory conversations they were engaged in made them feel uneasy. Students from across racial and theological contexts were forced to navigate presuppositions resulting from their enculturated theological norms. No student walked away fully comfortable. The experience did three things for students: it facilitated appreciation for an expression of Christianity that many had previously written off; it forced students to articulate their objections in ways they had never been asked to before; and it opened the door to flexibility with what some of the students had previously seen as nonnegotiables within their faith. Through it all, the students benefitted by engaging with a theological community that pressed them outside of their comfort zones.

Examination and Credentialing

Many students are wondering about the necessity and relevance of formal credentialing. Ordination is facilitated by a wide variety of means in the US. In many nondenominational and independent churches, the leadership body ordains ministers without much process, and the ordination is rescinded when a person's service to the church is finished. Ordination and credentialing, however they exist in the community and theological tradition in which you would like to serve, are largely a product of the particularities of that congregation or denominational connection.

It is important to find a theological home in the process of your theological studies. As stifling as it may seem, exploring general denominational frameworks is important. Some students are commissioned by a denomination before beginning their studies. Some may question their commitment after being exposed to a wider range of traditions. Other students may come from non-denominational settings and discover that despite the "non" descriptor, their church sits within as firm a theological or political tradition and framework as any formal denomination. Like every other theological family, nondenominational churches have roots in particular ideologies and thinkers and espouse the ministerial values of those that came before them.

You want to avoid investing in a church with a tradition that will not allow you to be your full self or minister with your conscience intact. Most denominations have theological cousins that allow some flexibility and movement.

Recent theological questions over LGBTQ+ inclusion, weddings, and clergy ordination have left many confused about their denominational ties, without a denominational home, or with a feeling of cynicism about the efficacy of the institutional church moving forward. Nothing can prepare you to engage this season of the church's history like a robust theological education. It is a sobering responsibility, for example, when a young person (or the parents of one), a colleague, a friend, or someone identifying as LGBTQ+ comes to you asking what you believe about the state of the person's soul. You will ease your own soul in the face of these questions by standing on a solid foundation. In such moments, your confidence and authenticity will be invaluable, especially when they are supplemented by a theological education that has prepared you for the hermeneutical, historical, and missional implications of issues you will encounter.

Choosing a denomination or theological family allows you a place where you can stand amid the messy and gray parts of ministry. There is value in submitting yourself to the wisdom of people who have struggled through their own questions and dilemmas about how the Holy Spirit moved in their time. Most denominations were started by a reformer with an entrepreneurial spirit, but over time convictions became institutionalized and less responsive to current events and cultural shifts. Richard Rohr entreats us to engage these systems not from the outside but from "the edge of the inside." He writes that "only with great respect for and understanding of the rules can a prophet know how to properly break those very same rules—for the sake of a greater purpose and value. A prophet critiques a system by quoting its own documents, constitutions, heroes, and Scriptures against its present practice. This is their secret: systems are best unlocked from inside."[69]

69. Rohr, "Edge."

There is no right or wrong choice when it comes to whether the Holy Spirit leads you to engage a denominational system from "the edge of the inside" or to forge a trail without the baggage and trappings of an institution. Either way, we are linked to the good and bad things that our predecessors have done in the name of Christ. We inherit a complicated history of the church as it relates to society. Christianity has an amazing heritage of service to society through the ministry of hospitals, educational institutions, nonprofit disaster-relief organizations, and poverty eradication programs. We also inherit a form of Christianity that has violated its foundation by baptizing violence in the name of Christ, perpetuating white supremacy, and committing spiritual and physical abuse. Whether we like it or not, these failures are well known and acutely remembered by a rapidly secularizing culture.

A practical case for ordination can be made. Being tethered to a wider group of churches and ministers can assure the security of resources and provide a built-in community of accountability. Most formal ordination processes are focused on discernment and on making sure you are prepared and well-matched for the vocation you seek. I (Doug) started the ordination process in the same denomination in which I'd spent all of my adult years to that point. Though the process took longer than I anticipated, it ultimately went rather smoothly and has served me well since then.

On the other hand, I (Jess) have been through three ordination processes in less than twenty years of ministry as I have evolved as a theological being. The processes have ranged widely. The first process was largely a formality. It included a one-time sit-down with a church elder board in the context of the strong relationships that had resulted from our having done ministry together. The second process involved a year's worth of reading, written doctrinal statements, and mentoring. The third is an exhaustive process that has taken colleagues up to ten years to complete. Engaging a religious bureaucracy of any size takes faith. This faith can pay off as you share your ministry life with a family of discernment and support—even if you find yourself advocating for change from "the edge of the inside."

Process, Not Perfection

No one is expected to perfect the shaping tools of spiritual disciplines during their theological education experience, in their first
years in ministry, or even through a lifetime of service. However,
it would be great for you to begin to cultivate these means of grace
while in school. They will enhance your study, serve as a connection point to God while you grapple with new ideas, and most
likely remain a part of your life in the years that follow. No one
gets into prime physical shape by reading kinesiology textbooks.
No one becomes an amazing chef by watching cooking shows. You
will not embody Mother Teresa's compassion for the marginalized
or the holiness to which Paul entreats us by waiting until after
graduation. Small, regular actions can get you on the road.

When we think of spiritual practices, the image that often
comes to mind is one of sequestered men and women of the past in
cloisters whose "work" is the cultivation of prayer. Few of us today
have the luxury to learn spirituality within a monastic framework.
The shaping tools that sustain our work need to be cultivated and
to evolve in our ever-changing world.

The Scandrette family leads a community of spiritual experimentation in the San Francisco area. Having located themselves
in a creative city, members of the family have chosen a creative
methodology for spiritual development. Mark Scandrette gathers
together committed Christians, marginal church attendees, and
individuals antagonistic to the faith, and engages them together
in spiritual practices. These temporary spiritual experimentations
are often art- or justice-related and geared toward awakening the
life of the Spirit through positive risk. His groups have taken steps
to purge excess and give to the poor, prophetically engaged the sex
industry in Mark's San Francisco neighborhood, and brought out
the healing qualities of art for persons situated across a diversity of
religious backgrounds.

Scandrette asserts that spiritual growth happens through
embodied doing: "Transformation happens through new experiences. . . . When we risk going to new places, meeting new people,

and risking new activities the resulting disequilibrium can create space for change. New experiences challenge our assumptions and beliefs, help us face our fears and surprise us with resources and strength we didn't know we had."[70]

We can learn from this embodied pedagogy. The spirituality promoted by the Scandrettes is never seen as a pass/fail venture. It profoundly reacts to the lived experiences of neighbors. It is highly relational and accessible. The Scandrettes' liturgical communities practice confession without judgment while intentionally getting outside of comfort zones. Scandrette remarks on our propensity to catalog the things we give up in order to practice "works of piety." But he reframes the question in a way that helps us cultivate the means of grace that we have outlined in this chapter. Scandrette writes that "rather than begrudgingly asking, 'What do I have to do?' or 'How far do I have to go?' a better question is, 'How free and alive am I willing to be?'"[71] We have the opportunity to live into the fullness of our lives as creatures created by a living and loving God. We have the ability to live in amazing freedom, nurtured by the care and guidance of the Spirit.

Crafting a Rule of Life

When it comes to practicing the shaping tools of spiritual disciplines, most people will discover that good intentions are not enough. Life is full of responsibilities and distractions, and adding school classes and assignments to the mix only intensifies the pressure of one's daily schedule. A rule of life—an intentional rhythm of living that incorporates particular tools and practices—can be like a trellis, providing the structure needed to "curb our tendency to wander and support our frail efforts to grow spiritually."[72] We can find numerous examples of life rules, both communal and individual, in the Christian tradition. The Rule of St. Benedict is

70. Scandrette, *Practicing*, 77.

71. Scandrette, *Practicing*, 47.

72. Thompson, *Soul Feast*, 138.

an example of a formal, communal rule of life that has governed daily and spiritual life in many monasteries since the sixth century. More recently, Martin Luther King Jr. required each volunteer under his leadership in Birmingham, Alabama, to sign a commitment card and pledge themselves to the "ten commandments" of the nonviolent movement. These commandments comprised a rule of life that directed activists to "meditate daily on the teachings and life of Jesus," "pray daily to be used by God in order that all might be free," and "seek to perform regular service for others and for the world."[73]

Ruth Hailey Barton prefers the language of "rhythm" when it comes to crafting a personal rule of life, because "it speaks of regularity that the body and soul can count on, but it also speaks of ebb and flow, creativity and beauty, music and dancing, joy and giving ourselves over to a force or a power that is beyond ourselves and is deeply good."[74] She suggests that we begin by listening to our longings and asking ourselves the question, "How do I want to live so I can be who I want to be?"[75] It may be useful to "try" spiritual disciplines out, one at a time, to discern which are most important for your current formation and how they might be practically incorporated into your life. An effective rule of life will be ruthlessly realistic: concrete and specific, as well as balanced and flexible.[76] Thinking in terms of daily, weekly, seasonal, and yearly rhythms can help you craft a manageable rule, which you should periodically reevaluate and "retool," especially if you experience significant life transitions. Don't keep your rule secret; asking a spiritual companion or small group to hold you accountable can mean the difference between intention and execution. If you are artistic or musical, you could even create a visual or aural representation of your rule to help you remember it and live it out.

Throughout this chapter, we've frequently employed the words *work*, *tools*, and *practice* as we have described the journeyman/

---

73. King, *Why We Can't Wait*, 63–64.

74. Barton, *Sacred Rhythms*, 147–48.

75. Barton, *Sacred Rhythms*, 147.

76. Barton, *Sacred Rhythms*, 148–52.

woman stage of vocational ministry. It is true, as we stated in the introduction to the chapter, that becoming a master of your craft will involve "daily, and sometimes tedious, labor." However, we want to conclude by emphasizing that these words do not tell the whole story. As we read the testimonies of Christians who persevered at mastering the tools of ministry, there's another reality that is present: the themes of beauty, joy, and delight. Our Master is the source and Creator of all that is beautiful and good, and as we are shaped into Christ's image, we will participate in that beauty and goodness and joy. In fact, the shaping disciplines themselves often become vehicles to joy and delight. St. Teresa of Ávila struggles to find words to describe the rapture she experiences in God's presence, when "labor is accompanied by so much bliss and comfort to the soul that the soul would never willingly abandon it."[77] Howard Thurman writes about "the magic, the spell of love" which "blesses a life with a vision of its possibilities never before dreamed of or sought, stimulating new endeavor and summoning all latent powers to energize the life at its inmost core."[78] We are apprenticed to the One who is an expert at making "all things new" and bringing beauty out of ashes,[79] and there is joy in the daily journey of learning this trade.

Backstory Four—Holistic Challenges to the Modern Compartmentalization of Theological Education

In the early church, those who prepared for ministry sat under the tutelage of well-established clergy who worked with them in a person-to-person fashion. The pastoral training model for medieval priests included the apprenticeship of ministers-to-be at monasteries, cathedral schools, or church-based universities. Spiritual formation through regular times of prayer and devotion, often conducted under a rule of precepts, accompanied the medieval

77. Teresa of Ávila, *Life*, 122.

78. Thurman, *Inward Journey*, 185.

79. Rev 21:5; Isa 61:3.

students' biblical and theological studies. The shaping tools of the spiritual disciplines worked in tandem with the forming tools of the intellectual disciplines.

Only during the modern period (after 1650 or so) did theological education become lodged in institutions (colleges, universities, and seminaries) that weren't immediately connected with the day-to-day life of a parish or worship setting. Then, after 1810, the ministerial preparation program that developed at the University of Berlin became preeminent (as described in the Backstory in chapter 3). In the Berlin model, theological instruction occurred at a university unaffiliated with any local congregation. The intellectual development of the student took precedence over spiritual formation and practical experience.

Philipp Spener's 1675 suggestion, then, that theological schools should be "nurseries of the church" and "workshops of the Holy Spirit"—that is, places where students are oriented congregationally and shaped devotionally—cut against the grain of the educational principles advanced by his modern contemporaries. The compartmentalization of intellectual scholarship away from faith formation and the regular rhythm of congregational worship has dominated modern theological education. But at numerous times during the modern era, challengers have arisen and defied the predominant paradigm. These challengers have provided bold examples of relevant and formative educational experiences for those called into ministry.

Spener himself furnished one of the earliest examples—first, by his book-length summons to the church, entitled *Pia Desideria*, or "Pious Hopes." In the book, he challenged Christian leaders to provide common sense ways for people to become more faithful, such as lay-led Bible studies, small cell groups for devotional renewal, and practical, down-to-earth sermons. Second, Spener helped to start a more spiritually oriented school for educating pastors. The school, known as the University of Halle in eastern Germany, trained hundreds of Pietist pastors. Halle actually became a "workshop of the Holy Spirit" along the lines that Spener envisioned.[80]

80. Spener, *Pia Desideria*, 17–22; Stein, *Philipp Jakob Spener*, 130–33.

Several other examples of institutions can be named that have challenged the modern separation between the academic study of theology on the one hand and Christian devotion and worship on the other. For instance, Spener's protégé, Nicholas von Zinzendorf, formed a spiritual community at Herrnhut in Saxony that eventually sent pastors and missionaries all over the world. Zinzendorf's Spirit-led religious group, called the Moravians, strongly influenced the brothers John and Charles Wesley, who in turn established the Kingswood School in Bristol, England. Kingswood championed the bringing together of reasoned belief with affective experience. To cite the aspirational wording of the Wesleys' dedicatory hymn for the school, they committed themselves to "unite the pair so long disjoined, knowledge and vital piety." Such "learning and holiness combined" became a watchword for many subsequent educational ventures.[81]

Over the years, poor or oppressed Christian groups on the fringes of genteel society found themselves excluded from the high-brow academic culture typical of most mainline churches. Some examples of these marginalized groups include Christian abolitionists, people from the Holiness movement, Pentecostals, African American Christians, Appalachian Christians, and members of Latin American base communities. These groups frequently started their own schools or training programs, in which they melded biblical study, spiritual formation, character development, and (in the case of the nineteenth-century abolitionists at Oberlin College and Berea College, and in today's base communities) direct action for social justice.[82]

In yet another example of defiance to the predominant educational norm, Bonhoeffer trained pastors-to-be from the Confessing (anti-Fascist) Church from 1935 to 1937 at a remote location in the small town of Finkenwalde. This illegal seminary became a place of spiritual respite for young pastors, many of whom would later be martyred by the Nazi government. Bonhoeffer insisted that the Finkenwalde seminary community worship

81. Wesley, *Hymns*, no. 40.
82. Dayton and Strong, *Rediscovering*, 85–105; Cook, *Expectation*.

together every day, often singing African American spirituals that Bonhoeffer had learned at The Abyssinian Baptist Church in Harlem when he had studied years before in New York City. They also practiced other spiritual shaping tools, such as prayer, solitude, and regular meals together. Bonhoeffer wrote his reflections on the privilege of Christian fellowship in community, which is now published as *Life Together* and has been a recurring source in these pages.[83] Although his experiences and writings are specific to his historical location and context, they can help us envision what it might look like to integrate both the framing and the shaping tools of theological formation in our own time and place.

83. Bonhoeffer, *Life Together.*

5

Becoming a Master

Honing the Craft of Ministry as the
Spirit Creates a Masterpiece

CRAFTSPEOPLE EXPEND MUCH TIME and effort producing exqui-
site artistic creations. As apprentices they invest energy and commitment over the long haul. Then, after they immerse themselves
in challenging and rewarding labor for many years, they're given
an opportunity to progress from being apprentices to becoming
masters in their own right. Artisans can earn the privilege of becoming masters when they develop their skills to such an extent
that they're identified as experts in their crafts.[1]

The progression toward mastery in an occupation is a reality
for theologians, clergy, chaplains, and other ministers, as well as
artisans. Theologians and their ilk participate in their own type
of apprenticeship as they engage in the craft of ministry. The craft
of ministry may include pastoral care, preaching, community
involvement, justice advocacy, evangelism, careful study of the
Bible and the church's tradition, and digging deeply into other
theological topics. Both the academy and the church have determined specific ways to signify when theologians, be they located

---

1. See note 2 in chapter 1 for a description of the word *master* as that term
was used in the medieval guilds and is still used by some craftspeople today.

in theological schools or in pastoral ministry, exhibit mastery of their craft. For instance, when graduate-level theological students demonstrate mastery over biblical exegesis, church history, and the other varied subjects that they've studied at their institution, they obtain a "master's" degree. And when theologically gifted pastors, after many seasons of effective preaching and teaching, demonstrate their mastery of the craft of ministry by serving as examples for other church leaders of how to do pastoral work well, they may be acknowledged by their congregations or denominations as a kind of "master" by receiving honorary titles or designations. This honoring of senior-level pastors occurs most frequently among African American churches, Korean American churches, and other churches of color. Through such acknowledgment, master pastors are recognized as skilled professionals in ministry.

Growth toward becoming a master doesn't happen spontaneously. As we've seen throughout this book, an extensive and detailed process guides apprentices on the path to excellence in their fields. Apprentices begin, for example, by studying under the tutelage of mentors and specialists, who have already shown proficiency in their crafts. These expert craftspeople might be weavers, potters, and blacksmiths, or in the theological arena, professors and experienced pastors (see chapter 1). Apprentices are also trained in the specific nuances of their crafts, whether weaving, pottery, and smithing or the study of theological doctrines, biblical exegesis, and ministry praxis. They've become adept at knowing the peculiarities of the medium of their crafts, whether those be fabric, clay, and iron, or the context of a congregation's community (see chapter 2). They've determined that they need to depend on the camaraderie and teamwork of other apprentices, which in the case of ministry includes other pastors, ministry leaders, and theologians (see chapter 3). And they've practiced with tools especially appropriate for their crafts. The tools that they use may be framing tools such as looms, potters' wheels, and anvils, or the theological framing tools of learning the biblical narrative, church history, and systematic theology. Other tools of their trade may be shaping tools, such as shuttles, jiggers, and chisels, or the spiritual shaping tools of prayer, meditation on Scripture, and mutual accountability (see chapter 4).

The many hours spent in the workshop provide a setting for artisans to hone their skills, allowing them eventually to develop their capabilities to such a degree that they can become masters in their own shops. The same type of procedure operates in the realm of theology. Your theological education, for instance, is part of a process of honing skills in the craft of ministry. You may be earning an undergraduate or graduate degree from your college, seminary, or university, in one of the subject areas of theology, religion, biblical studies, or ministry. On the undergraduate level, such degrees are known as "bachelor's" degrees. A bachelor in medieval times was a junior member of a guild, and so we can say that one who receives a bachelor's degree in theology has begun his or her work in the guild of ministry. (Unfortunately, the term *bachelor* also reflects the antiquated and sexist understanding that the initial stage of higher education was reserved for younger, male students.) On the graduate level, one's theological education results in a master's degree in theology or divinity. The use of the term *master* reflects how the origin of degree-granting universities occurred in the same medieval milieu as the craft workshop. The student who is an apprentice in theology receives the title of master when she or he accomplishes mastery in theological study in the same way that an apprentice in silver craftwork, for example, accomplishes mastery as a silversmith and thereby earns the title of master in that field.

To become a master at anything, including theological study and ministry, takes hard work and a strict regimen. Descriptions of workshop culture often emphasize the skill of the individual craftsperson. Indeed, the acquisition of a person's skills is absolutely necessary. Blacksmiths must sharpen their dexterity in metalworking; potters must spend years perfecting their ability to shape ceramics at the wheel; and theologians must fine-tune their pastoral sensitivity and their exegetical aptitude.

Skills development, however, is never accomplished alone. As we've described in this book, artisanal tasks are always accomplished in a shop alongside others, and the shops together are part of guilds. The craftwork of a textile worker, glassblower, or cooper—or a pastor or theological student—can never be done adequately by oneself. We cannot stress that enough. In the workshop of the Holy Spirit, we need each other in order to flourish in our callings. The synergy that comes from many people working together enhances the quality of the product of our labor.

An interesting example of jointly produced tasks is the work associated with Eastern Orthodox Christians who create icons to be used for religious devotion. Although icons are said to be "written," rather than painted, they are nonetheless produced in a shop or studio like other crafts. Generally speaking, we don't know the names of iconographers (icon writers), since icons are written collaboratively and anonymously by religiously committed, professional artisans, often monks. Even the most famous Russian Orthodox iconographer of all time, the early fifteenth-century artist Andrei Rublev, did not sign his own icons. He worked alongside other monks at a workshop in his monastery of Trinity-St. Sergius near Moscow. Consequently, there came to be an entire Rublevian school of icon writing. Because his order of monks produced icons collectively, we aren't sure which specific icons Rublev himself painted (wrote) and which ones were created by his students. The products of the entire studio together reflect the superb style and careful workmanship of Andrei Rublev.[2]

We can also see the importance of collaborative witness within the biblical canon. For instance, at the conclusion of John's Gospel, the text reads like this: "This [John] is the disciple who is testifying to these things and has written them, and we know that his testimony is true."[3] Who are the "we" who know that John's testimony of the Gospel account is true? Those corroborating his testimony were unnamed members of John's community who attested to the credibility of the message. Like the followers of John, theological students and pastoral leaders need one another to stay focused and to substantiate the truthfulness of our shared testimony.

2. Bittner, *Masterpieces*, 20–27.

3. John 21:24.

No one is self-made or self-sufficient. No one is autonomous. You may have a home church to rely on during your theological studies, or your family, or relationships from your internship or field education site. All those networks are good, and it's especially crucial for you to be connected to a church or other fellowship group near where you live during your studies. But the folks in your church or your family probably aren't reading what you're reading or being exposed to the theological challenges that you're experiencing. Consequently, along with those important support structures, it's also vital for you to find ways to experience a sense of community with those with whom you're studying. You may need to take the initiative to create such a community for yourself. Since I (Doug) traveled far away from my family and home church when I went to theological school, my experience of seminary would've been very isolating without a small group of peers—fellow students who prayed with me and encouraged me. We formed the group during our first year of study after it became evident that we were all concerned that we were spiritually adrift. It sustained me during those years, and I've found that if anything, the need for such fellowship becomes greater when one leaves school and encounters the demanding and often lonesome challenges of ministry.

Apprenticing with the Master Spirit

Even more essential than our fellowship with colleagues is the practice of remaining closely tethered to God in our ministry and theological education. Dependence on God's grace should be the distinguishing mark of our ministry praxis and theological study. When Philipp Spener wrote that theological academies ought to be viewed as workshops of the Holy Spirit, he meant that every individual participating in the academy is being trained by the Spirit—the true Master. In such a workshop, Spener proposed, it's the Spirit who mentors all the people at the school, both students and professors. Everyone in the theological workshop remains as an apprentice in relation to the Master Spirit.

The very title of *professor*, for instance, refers to a person in any subject area who "professes"—that is, a person who affirms, acknowledges, or declares allegiance to that area of study. First and foremost, then, a professor believes in something (or someone), and then she teaches out of that belief. Christian professors in the Spirit's workshop are not very different from their students, at least in this way, for both learners and teachers are "professing" believers who are equally under God's guidance. The only significant difference between Spirit-led students and Spirit-led professors in the theological workshop is that professors have more time and experience under their belts, which enables them to speak confidently and authoritatively, yet humbly, from the perspective of that experience.

This combination of confidence and humility is a biblical value for anyone who teaches and preaches God's Word—not just theological professors, but all who study theology and everyone who puts on the mantle of ministry for the church. Even after you receive a bachelor's or master's degree, for instance, the one in charge of the workshop of your ministry will still be the Holy Spirit. That's the cosmic chuckle that God will utter at the end of your education: "Guess what, my friend? After all this academic work, you're not actually the master of anything—and certainly not of yourself or your workplace!"

The importance of modesty is particularly true for those who are studying to become masters of *divinity*. Isn't that a pretentious claim? It seems very grandiose, quite frankly, to assert that someone can master being divine. Nonetheless, that's the traditional term used for the degree, and so it's probably a good practice for all of us in theological education to realize and repeat to ourselves frequently that we won't be able to come anywhere near to divinity until by grace we are glorified in God's presence.

The acknowledgment that we need to be humble in our role as proclaimers of God's Word is made clear in the third chapter of the epistle of James, where we read a very ominous-sounding admonition: "Not many of you should become teachers, my brothers and sisters, for you know that we who teach will be judged with greater strictness."[4] James is saying that although the roles of teacher and preacher are awesome they're also fraught with great responsibility and obligation, since those of us in such roles are entrusted with the intellectual, emotional, and spiritual health of others.

Thankfully, James's cautionary and somewhat intimidating warning is followed immediately by this statement: "For all of us make many mistakes."[5] This verse assumes that professors and pastors will sometimes mess up. You may think that the assertion that theologians and pastors are prone to error is a self-evident observation! But what if everyone were to make this honest admission—that "all of us make many mistakes" as teachers and preachers? And what if we took seriously the implication that follows from owning our tendency to mess up? That is, what if we readily admitted our proclivity to fail? It might lead us to depend more thoroughly on the promptings of the Spirit rather than on our vaunted opinions or educational credentials.

Derick was raised in an historic African American Baptist congregation. He came to faith in Jesus Christ early in life and received spiritual mentoring from his church's longtime, seasoned pastor, who also served as a father figure for Derick. At the age of sixteen, Derick felt a profound call from the Lord to become an ordained pastor. He began preaching regularly and led a ministry to other youth. Derick's zeal for God was contagious. Following college, and then after some time as a youth pastor and evangelistic speaker, Derick was admitted to a prestigious theological school. Off he went, full of earnest enthusiasm.

Derick did not anticipate the intellectual snobbery, racist microaggressions, cynicism toward the church, or privileged presumptions that often characterize elite, white, mainline Christianity, especially at some theological schools. His defense against this mental and spiritual onslaught was to knuckle down academically and become a sharp and thoughtful questioner in the front row of every classroom. He obtained exceptional grades and the accolades of his professors while debating any fellow student who

4. Jas 3:1.
5. Jas 3:2.

chose to oppose him. Passion for God morphed into a passion for theological one-upmanship.

Derick adapted in order to survive emotionally. In the process, though, he felt increasingly detached and nearly lost his soul. Worship became infrequent, God became an abstraction, and ministry became a well-rehearsed performance. The firm, strong cord of his faith in Christ seemed to be reduced to just a slender thread, and he wasn't sure whether he could hang on.

After graduation, Derick returned home and gradually recovered his spiritual grip, including a deep love for God, ministry, and the church. But now Derick interprets his time spent in theological education as a cautionary tale for others who are about to embark on that journey. While Derick's season at seminary was distinct, it unfortunately wasn't unique. He is grateful for the education he received. His experience, however, provides testimony to the truth that none of us, neither students nor professors, are immune to the seductive gazes of success, achievement, and notoriety—and that even the most well-intentioned theological communities can unknowingly create unwelcome and hurtful environments for those who attempt to join them. That's why all of us, students and teachers alike, need the continual accountability of the community of faith in Jesus *outside* the academy to bear prophetic witness in love when we stray from living the very best of the Gospel's message of reconciliation and self-giving service among each other. All who profess the Christian faith need to be grounded in the reality of ecclesial communities, not cordoned off into the corners of the academy.

This has always been the charge of Christ's church: how do we translate what we're learning into the day-to-day life of the people we serve? How do we recognize that justice and holiness can become hollow concepts if they're not predicated on the experiences of a living, breathing community? We need the tangible witness of church folks to speak into our education.

It's important to note the essential nature of discernment on the part of students and professors alike as they labor in the workshop of the Spirit. It's an unfortunate fact that, in a fallen world, not all theological influence from peers and faculty is created equal. Some members of a theological institution, for example, may seem only interested in deconstruction, which can result in a kind of self-congratulatory agnosticism or seeming spiritual sophistication at best, and theological nihilism at worst. Those forces can injure the spiritual growth of students and faculty and the parishes that they will serve. Craftspeople in the Spirit's workshop must be accountable to a community for insight to know what is true, good, and beautiful, and what is not. On the whole, the influence of the master craftspeople you encounter will be extremely fruitful for your ministry, for the church, and for the world. But it's worth acknowledging that discernment in the Spirit within the body of Christ Jesus will be necessary as you remain faithful to the truth of God's self-revealed nature during your theological education and your service in ministry.

In 1675, Spener wrote that any theological student "who fervently loves God, although adorned with limited gifts, will be more useful to the church of God with his meager talent and academic achievement than a vain and worldly fool with double doctor's degrees who is very clever but has not been taught by God. The work of the former is blessed, and he is aided by the Holy Spirit. The latter has only a carnal knowledge, with which he can easily do more harm than good."[6] Spener knew that competence in the craft of ministry comes from much more than just scholarly proficiency in the study of theology; it also comes from our love from God and for God, as shaped through the church. When we ground our endeavors on those love relationships, we're "aided by the Holy Spirit" in our work.

Relying on the Spirit

But what will it mean to be aided by the Holy Spirit in your work as a theological student? How can you remain cognizant of God's grace throughout your time spent in an academic environment? In

6. Spener, *Pia Desideria*, 108.

what ways can you envision the Holy Spirit as the true Master of your theological education?

Relying on the Spirit as our Master means, in the first place, that we can rest in the Spirit's embrace and trust in the Spirit's guidance. Jesus describes how *the Spirit's ongoing presence with us* attests to divine assistance for his followers. In John 14, Jesus promises his disciples that although he would be departing from their physical presence, the Father "will give you another Helper."[7] This Helper—sometimes translated as Advocate, Comforter, or Companion—is the Greek word *paraclete*, which means "one who stands beside." "The Helper, the Holy Spirit," Jesus says, "will teach you all things, and bring to your remembrance all that I said to you."[8] When we truly depend on the Spirit, we can trust that no matter what we're learning about in our theological education—whether it seems enlightening, exhilarating, intoxicating, and imaginative, or confusing, difficult, troubling, and uprooting—the Spirit of Jesus will be our enduring companion, teaching us all things necessary for remaining faithful in our walk with God.

Though the Holy Spirit takes the lead, our connection with the Spirit is a reciprocal relationship. The Spirit brings Jesus' teachings to our remembrance, and then we in turn lean into the Spirit for our strength, confidence, and wisdom for discernment. This spiritual respiration, a kind of breathing of God's presence, fosters in us a pattern of continual reliance on the Spirit, the true Master-teacher. And in order to experience this respiratory interaction persistently and find ourselves routinely attuned to the Holy Spirit, we may need to develop a more consistent use of the spiritual shaping tools described in the previous chapter.

Along with having a close trust in God's immanent presence via the Spirit's companionship, there is a second way in which we can rely on the Holy Spirit as the Master of our theological education. Depending on the Spirit also allows us to be attentive to *the ways in which God breaks into our reality*. This awareness of the transcendent God entering into our lives—the infusion of

7. John 14:16 NASB.
8. John 14:26 NASB.

the Spirit's power—is what the philosopher Charles Taylor calls cracks in the "immanent frame." Taylor tells us that God is continually breaking in, stepping through the immanent frame of secularism. Only the transcendent initiative of the Spirit can fill the God-shaped hole in every one of us. Taylor finds God breaking in, for instance, through art—the transcendence recognizable in Wordsworth's poetry and Wagner's music. He argues that certain works of art (Dante, Bach, and the Chartres Cathedral, for example—and, we would add, the genius of artists such as Makoto Fujimura, Mary Oliver, and the composers of African American spirituals, among many other creative minds) evoke a power that seems inseparable from their transcendent reference.[9]

How does such an emphasis on God's inbreaking relate to our lives as students? In addition to being our Helper and Companion, God's Spirit can be seen as the one who inspires (literally "breathes into") our imagination and inventiveness. That is, the Spirit wants to be the ultimate source of originality in our learning. If we depend on the Spirit, we'll be open to God's interjection of new ideas and innovation into our theological study.

We can see this receptivity to God's creativity when we examine the ways in which the Spirit is depicted in Scripture. In the New Testament, the relevant Greek term is *pneuma*, a word that can refer to spirit or breath or wind. Throughout the New Testament, the Spirit, and not humanity, is the initial agent of action, for the *pneuma* "blows where it chooses."[10] In the Hebrew Bible, the parallel word *ruach* (also signifying spirit or breath) occurs 389 times. The varied instances of this term portray an animating presence that may be either invigorating or disquieting and sometimes both. But whichever way the word is used, God's *ruach* has the potential to shake us up. And Scripture attests to the fact that God's people frequently need to be shaken up!

James Loder became enamored with the social sciences in his graduate program at Harvard Divinity School. But then he had a

9. Taylor, *Secular Age*. The phrase "immanent frame" appears throughout Taylor's book.

10. John 3:8.

direct encounter with the Holy Spirit when he came face-to-face with his mortality during a harrowing, life-threatening traffic accident. This "transforming moment" forced Loder "to radically reconsider the very core of his self-understanding and the meaning of his life's vocation."[11] The accident became a genuine epiphany for Loder, leading him to recast his thinking. He changed his academic outlook from a psychoanalytic perspective to a theological one, even though his "turn to the Spirit" brought criticism from some of his scholarly colleagues. Loder spent his subsequent years as a Christian education professor at Princeton Theological Seminary, where he reclaimed the essential role of the Holy Spirit in discipleship, helping seminarians to move away from questions of content acquisition ("What do I know?") and toward questions about the ways in which they are invited to participate in God's mission ("What do I believe and do?").[12]

In contrast to James Loder's sensational Holy Spirit encounter, Renita Weems, formerly a professor and administrator at Vanderbilt Divinity School and American Baptist College, writes about "luminous moments that are otherwise quite unremarkable." At the edge of "everyday, ordinary, commonplace occasions comes an invitation from some irresistible force, by God, to come closer and listen more attentively. . . . It is precisely moments like these that leave me tripping up into my purpose, staggering into some insight I desperately need, and backing up into God."[13] Like Loder, Weems is recounting God-shaped, transforming moments. But in the "luminous" instances of spiritual intervention that Weems describes, the Spirit breaks through undramatically. Whether the moments are spectacular or more commonplace, God's Spirit persistently enters into our lives. God will empower your studying and your ministry with creativity, imagination, and transformation.

The Spirit's shaking up may apply to our theological schools as well as to us as individuals. When Spener used the metaphor of "workshops of the Holy Spirit," he linked two contrasting

11. Wright and Kuentzel, *Redemptive*, 15.
12. Loder, *Transforming*.
13. Weems, *Listening for God*, 48.

concepts to describe institutions for ministerial training: a workshop conjures up one type of image while the Holy Spirit elicits a very different type of image. A workshop, while sometimes messy, is nevertheless an environment that provides structure for one's work. Meanwhile, the Spirit's activity has the potential to be a free-wheeling or unpredictable presence in one's work. The combining of the two images suggests that there may be an inherent tension in theological education. That is, theological schools demonstrate institutional stability on the one hand and academic freedom on the other, emphasizing both human-made structure and an openness to the Spirit. Each is essential.

The tension between an ordered learning environment and divine inspiration is also felt within us as theological students. We flourish when we're given room to experience the Spirit's creative enabling but also when we have the guidance of an organized setting of mentored training. When we participate in the educational process that is provided by our schools, we may find ourselves oscillating between an impulse toward spontaneity and a corresponding impulse toward systematic regularity. This correspondence is not a negative thing, for the counterbalance of these two impulses, which we're calling the workshop of the Holy Spirit, can be precisely the space where we do our best and most rewarding work. Craftspeople thrive when they work both within the structure provided by their workshop and with the ingenuity of their artistic license. Likewise, theological students and ministers need the structure provided by their colleges, universities, seminaries, congregations, and denominations, along with the students' and ministers' inspired and intuitive insights.

We've seen that we can rely on the Holy Spirit to be the Master of our theological education, first as an ongoing companion, and second as a creative inspirer. Thirdly, we perceive the Spirit as a *signpost to the future reign of God.*

A reliance on the Spirit means that we envision a hope-filled future, a perspective desperately needed in today's environment of anxiety and fear. We see signposts of God's good reign. The new creation that has already begun to happen with Jesus' resurrection will come to completion when God makes the new heavens and the new earth and raises us to share in that newness. Imagine a future beyond what seems realistic to us now, a breaking in of God's future into our present time. We work within the earthly city, even if our ultimate hope is in the city to come, when heaven comes to earth. N. T. Wright states that "the new life of the Spirit . . . should produce radical transformation of behavior in the present life, anticipating the life to come even though we know we shall never be complete and whole until then."[14]

Hugh of St. Victor, a monk in the twelfth century, wrote about three forms of creative work: *opus Dei* (what God creates), *opus naturae* (what nature creates), and *opus artificis* (what humans create as artisans). Hugh also identified ways of "reading" or perceiving the things that are created. When reading our human creations, we may find that they're corrupted. There are dangers associated with unrestrained creation. Our human creative impulse can be positive or negative. Yet through Christ's incarnation, God can transform the things we create as humans through the new creation.[15]

Hugh's understanding can be applied to human creativity today, such as the way in which we perceive technological advances. We know that the results of technology can be destructive, but technology also extends our wisdom and can be an indicator of God's restorative work. Perhaps aspects of technology can be harnessed to be part of the transformation of creation that reconciles all human creativity to God and the natural world. This can help us to imagine the future that God has waiting for us.[16]

When we depend on the Holy Spirit to guide our work as ministry practitioners and theologians, we recognize God's ever-present immanence, God's creative transcendence, and the promise of God's good reign in the future. And participating in the divine workshop means that we acknowledge the Spirit as the Master whose stamp of authentication is placed on all our theological study and ministry activity.

14. Wright, *Surprised*, 221.
15. Paulus, "Forms of Creation."
16. Paulus, "Forms of Creation."

We Are God's Workmanship

Acknowledging that the Holy Spirit is the true Master of our theological education and the Master of whatever we do in our ministry helps to free us from the presumption of achievement orientation and careerism. Once the burden of hubris and self-importance is lifted, we start to develop the skills necessary to become effective in the craft of ministry so that we can work toward the fulfillment of God's reign to the best of our ability and without egoism. "We are [God's] workmanship," Paul writes, "created in Christ Jesus for good works."[17] In the large canvas of God's handiwork, we recognize ourselves to be people who are learning how to become masters (in a secondary sense) so that we may serve the Master (in the primary sense).

Becoming a master in ministry means that we view our work through an appropriate lens—as God's work, not ours. That is, we consider ministry from God's perspective rather than from society's. The culture around us sees the pastorate or other ministry position as similar to any other job, and because of highly publicized scandals, perhaps a suspicious job at that. When we view our work in such a narrow way, as just a job or merely a pathway to the next career move, we may find ourselves overly concerned about things like salary, accolades, and recognition. This achievement orientation can easily lead to fatigue and burnout.

God, however, considers ministry differently. God views human work, whether in professional ministry or in the vocation of every believer, as one of the ways in which we participate in the new creation, cooperating with God in the divine mission (*missio Dei*) of restoring all people and the entire world to its original created glory. When we look at our work with that expansive perspective, we'll be much less prone to weariness and cynicism.

The distinctions among the different ways in which we perceive the work of ministry can be understood by studying the origins of the English words that we use to refer to occupations. Various terms function to describe the work (of any sort) that

17. Eph 2:10 NASB.

humans do. For the purposes of theological education, we can speak specifically about work within the church, broadly conceived, whether as a pastor or a nonprofit manager or a chaplain or a theological student or a professor or any other ministry role. Let's look at the etymological roots of the words *vocation* and *calling*, in contrast with the words *job* and *career*.

The word *vocation* came into the English language sometime before 1430, at the end of the medieval period. It's derived from the Latin word *vocatio*, meaning "a calling"—a spiritual calling from God. *Vocation* has the same root as the English word *voice*, as in the voice of God. *Calling*, in reference to an occupation, entered the English language even earlier, before 1250, and referred to "a summons to a way of life." It is derived originally from the Greek *kaleo*, "to call" or "to summon," and *kletos*, "to be called" or "to be invited." In short, God invites us and summons us to a life of faithfulness. This call of God on the entirety of our life is much bigger and more important than figuring out the specific way in which we're going to earn an income.

In the first chapter of Romans, Paul uses the Greek term *kletos* to talk about his own ministry and the ministry of believers: "Paul, a servant of Jesus Christ, called [*kletos*] to be an apostle, set apart for the gospel of God . . . the gospel concerning his Son . . . through whom we have received grace and apostleship to bring about the obedience of faith among all the Gentiles for the sake of his name, including yourselves who are called [*kletoi*] to belong to Jesus Christ."[18] Such a calling on our life is something already accomplished through Christ, something into which we already live. It's not something to be pursued as though we could achieve it through our own efforts. And what we're called into, most basically, is a growing relationship with the Trinity.

New words came into the English language during the modern era, when the means of production were changing, to describe the altered social reality that working people were experiencing. The word *job*, for example, appeared in English around 1557, referring to a task. It derived from the Middle English word *jobbe*, which

---

18. Rom 1:1, 3, 5–6.

meant a container, jar, or vase. By 1627, *job* had come to mean a piece of work. This meaning was extended to any piece of work or transaction done for pay or profit. Later, by 1699, the word signified anything that one had to do, any business or affair, and the means of work done for pay, a paid position, or general employment.

Similarly, the word *career* entered into the English language about 1534, right at the beginning of the modern period. It's derived from the French word *carrière*, which referred to a road for vehicles, a carriageway, a race course, or running at full speed, as in harness racing. The term has the same root as the English words *carriage* and *car*. The word acquired the sense of an occupation in 1803, through the writings of the Duke of Wellington, a successful politician and military field marshal who worked nonstop. To have a career, then, is to run in circles at full speed, or to compete against others on the figurative racetrack of one's workplace. Such a description sounds endlessly exhausting and depleting![19]

These words entered our language just prior to the time when Spener wrote his critique of modern trends in church life and the academy. The words represent exactly what Spener foresaw, and they anticipated what happened throughout European theological education, and in American theological education to some extent as well. That is, Spener was concerned that the study of religion as a compartmentalized subject among many other subjects at a university was replacing the study of theology (literally "an account of God") as an integrated aspect of a holistic life. Spener was fearful that a growing emphasis on the professionalism of ministry as a job would replace the long-established practice of ministry as a vocation.

Thankfully, instead of expecting followers of Jesus to perform at a job or to run after a career, the New Testament writers encourage us to enter our vocation as a summons to a way of life. As we read in the admonition given to young leaders in 1 Timothy, we are to "take hold of the life that really is life."[20]

---

19. Barnhart, *Chambers' Dictionary*, s.v. "job," "career," "vocation," and "calling."

20. 1 Tim 6:19.

Developing Mastery through Wisdom and Holiness

After we've determined who functions as the actual Master of the theological workshop, we can turn our attention to our process of becoming faithful and competent workers. What are the characteristics that we might expect to discover in us if through the power of the Spirit we become competent in the craft of ministry? How do we ascertain whether we've actualized mastery in our vocation? Biblical examples indicate that such mastery will be evident when we exhibit attributes of *wisdom* and *holiness*.

Wisdom repeatedly shows up in scriptural accounts as a gift from God received by people in conjunction with their efforts to carry out God-given tasks. The construction of the Hebrew tabernacle, for instance, provides a quintessential biblical illustration of the pursuit of expertise in craftwork on behalf of God. Notice how the quest for excellence is portrayed in the description of a temple craftsman named Bezalel:

> Now the LORD spoke to Moses, saying, "See, I have called by name Bezalel, the son of Uri. . . . I have filled him with the Spirit of God in wisdom, in understanding, in knowledge, and in all kinds of craftsmanship, to make artistic designs for work in gold, in silver, and in bronze, and in the cutting of stones for settings, and in the carving of wood, that he may work in all kinds of craftsmanship. . . . And in the hearts of all who are skillful I have put skill, that they may make all that I have commanded you."[21]

Through the Spirit, God provided Bezalel with understanding, knowledge, and "all kinds of craftsmanship." Bezalel's craft skills presumably took many years to perfect. Interestingly, though, God is declared to be the ultimate agent, even of the abilities that craftspeople develop themselves: "in the hearts of all who are skillful I have put skill." God's Spirit was with the skill of the temple craftsmen. For us in theological education, beyond the formal educational achievements of a degree, mastery will come after

21. Exod 31:1–6 NASB.

many years of practicing the craft of ministry in partnership with God's empowerment.

Along with the competence in artistic craftsmanship that was obtained through careful training, God also gave Bezalel wisdom. Indeed, wisdom is the first attribute named. In addition to the skillfulness that is expected of us and that comes through sustained training on our part, what will it mean for us to receive wisdom from God? What characterizes the wisdom that God bestows on us?

According to the book of Proverbs, in which wisdom is personified by using the metaphor of a craft workshop, wisdom induces imagination and lighthearted joy: "The LORD created me [wisdom] at the beginning of his work, the first of his acts of long ago. . . . When he marked out the foundations of the earth, then I was beside him, like a master worker; and I was daily his delight, rejoicing before him always, rejoicing in his inhabited world and delighting in the human race." The Common English Bible renders this passage with a playful translation: "I [wisdom] was beside him as a master of crafts. I was having fun . . . frolicking with his inhabited earth."[22]

The Scripture depicts God's wisdom embodying the identity of a skilled craftsperson who frolics with human beings. What a captivating and refreshing image! Wisdom delights and rejoices with us in our co-creative work with God. As theological students and ministry practitioners, we're encouraged to relish the inventive and aesthetic aspects of our vocation.

Wisdom encourages us to enjoy ministry while cultivating skillfulness. Spener wrote that a "reform of the church" will take place under the auspices of seasoned leaders who "have the divine wisdom to guide others carefully on the way of the Lord."[23] The skilled ministers who guide others carefully will foster emotional intelligence and a nuanced sense of self-awareness. Such skillfulness may include a posture of pliability. The wise practitioner will also deepen soft skills such as caring, empathy, boldness, patience,

22. Prov 8:22, 29–31 NRSV; 8:30–31 CEB.
23. Spener, *Pia Desideria*, 103.

balance, and enthusiasm. These skills are necessary because ministry professionals are often allowed into people's vulnerable spaces. How extraordinarily precious and daunting it is that ministers are invited into the best and worst moments of others' lives.

Wilbur Pollock, the beloved, unassuming pastor of my (Doug's) small-town home church, gained the confidence of the entire community during his many years of service to the congregation. People in our village trusted him with their deepest problems. They knew he would take their concerns seriously and hold their confidences tightly. Once, while visiting my hometown on break from seminary, I asked Pastor Pollock, "Would you let me in on the secret to your highly successful ministry?" Embarrassed by my compliment, he almost brushed aside my question, but eventually he offered me a simple, one-line maxim that I received as a summary statement to describe his effective pastorate: "Preach the gospel forthrightly and love the people unconditionally." Pastor Pollock demonstrated the masterful wisdom of delighting in and rejoicing with God and God's people.

Along with wisdom, another attribute given to us by God as we devote ourselves toward mastery in ministry is holiness. In Scripture, Christian leaders are repeatedly described as, or at least exhorted to be, people who live in a holy and sanctified manner. But how are we to understand holiness? Certainly not as a state of sinless perfection that we can acquire by our own efforts. Rather than being some kind of accomplished attainment, our knowledge of the craft of ministry grows and continues during a lengthy span of service, so that mastery is an ever-developing dynamism. Envision your vocation as moving on from your formal academic experiences to a lifetime of ministry. What will sustain you? What will help you to persist in doing well?

Over the long haul, what keeps us going is that God is moving us incrementally toward fullness and wholeness—the forging of a kind of spiritual skillfulness. Holiness, or sanctification, is the action of the Spirit that brings us to godly maturity through years of disciplined instruction. "The mature," says the writer of Hebrews, are "those whose faculties have been trained by practice."[24] Mastery comes from listening for and discerning the voice of God.

In the New Testament, the Greek term *hoi hagioi* is translated as "holy people" or "saints" or "those who have been made holy" and refers to those who are consecrated and dedicated to God. The term implies an association with the Holy Spirit and a continuous, growing relationship with God.

Intriguingly, the "holy people" mentioned in New Testament texts aren't usually described as actually living in a holy manner. In 1 Corinthians, for example, Paul addresses those in "the church of God that is in Corinth," along with "all those who in every place call on the name of our Lord Jesus Christ," and are "called to be saints."[25] Likewise, in 2 Corinthians, Paul describes the people who are receiving his letter as "the church of God that is in Corinth, including all the saints throughout Achaia."[26] (Achaia in Paul's day was the province that included the city of Corinth.) But Paul then goes on to describe those same Corinthian people who were "called to be saints" as having rivalries, sexual immorality, lawsuits against one another, and controversies over dress, spiritual gifts, and meat sacrifices.[27] Clearly they weren't acting very virtuously!

Similarly, in Colossians, Paul writes to "the saints and faithful brothers and sisters in Christ in Colossae,"[28] even though in the next chapter he criticizes the Colossian church for its participation in gnostic-related doctrines and religious practices. Scripture shows that the folks designated as saints are not always saintly.

Rather than an accomplished status, then, holiness is a goal toward which we're reaching. Sanctification is the fulfillment of a promise from God that we haven't yet attained. In this view of sanctification, instead of an achieved standing or a plateau at which we've arrived, our holiness is an increasing trajectory like the flight

---

24. Heb 5:14.
25. 1 Cor 1:2.
26. 2 Cor 1:1.
27. See 1 Cor 1:10–16; 5:1–2; 6:1–8; 7:1–16; 8:1–16; 12:1–11.
28. Col 1:2.

of an arrow right after it's been shot from the bow of the archer.[29] Christians seek the Spirit's power in order to be made holy—full of God's love toward God and others. But the sanctifying work of God is ongoing, not finished. To return to the workshop metaphor, even after craftspeople become masters at their trade, they still grow in the knowledge and skill of their craft over time.

Another aspect of the New Testament concept of holiness is that you can't be a saint by yourself. Christians need one another in order to be sanctified. In the seventeen New Testament uses of the term *hoi hagioi* (fourteen of them in the Pauline corpus), the phrase always appears in the plural. The term never occurs in the singular. Not once is a solitary "saint" mentioned—only many "saints" who are called to live out their lives together as Jesus' followers. Holiness, like mastery in ministry, doesn't come from being a lone-ranger believer; it occurs in community.

Producing a Masterpiece

To become a master, an apprentice had to submit a piece of work to the guild for evaluation. The apprentice produced a *magnum opus* ("great work") of high quality to obtain membership in his or her respective field of arts or crafts. This work, a masterpiece, demonstrated that the apprentice had achieved mastery of the craft. The masterpiece was required to be an exceptionally fine example of creative work so that the aspirant could be recognized as a master craftsperson. The guild judged the person's fitness to qualify for membership partly by the quality of the masterpiece, and if the applicant was successful, the guild retained ownership of the masterpiece.

To make a masterpiece, an artisan takes raw materials and shapes them with great care into something beautiful or useful. The piece created by the master-to-be reflects the distinct gifts and ingenuity of the person creating it. Martin Luther wrote that

---

29. The simile is not perfect, since the effect of gravity on an arrow will eventually cause it to descend.

"the work never makes the workman like itself, but the workman makes the work like himself."[30]

What is the masterpiece that we're creating as theologians or pastors in the craft of ministry? The masterpiece is our lived experience of ministry. Like expert weavers or potters, we generate fine, exceptional handiwork. Master craftspeople don't make mass-produced widgets and master ministers don't make cookie-cutter Christians. We disciple precious, one-of-a-kind people of faith. In the workshop, every piece—and even more so, every masterpiece—displayed uniqueness. Likewise, our service among Christ's body enhances the flourishing of each believer. And if ministry is our masterpiece, then the Holy Spirit retains it like the guild retained a craft masterpiece; we don't get to take credit for the ministry we accomplish. The work we do is for the sake of God's good reign.

We've said that ministry is a craft. Consequently, we have the privilege of creating a masterpiece derived from the fruits of our ministry. But perhaps we've been speaking about the analogy of a masterpiece incorrectly. There's another way to conceive of that metaphor. Instead of us being the object of agency for creating a masterpiece, perhaps we're the subject. Is ministry our masterpiece or are we the Spirit's masterpieces?

Perhaps your ministry isn't the craft. Perhaps *you* are the craft of the Holy Spirit. Indeed, God has already produced a masterpiece in each of us. In the early use of the word *masterpiece*, the term was often applied to humanity as God's *tour de force*. The Torah declares that God pronounced the creation of human beings "in God's own image" to be "supremely good." The psalmist proclaims that people are "fearfully and wonderfully made."[31] We're designed to be living, breathing bits of the new creation. The Spirit has formed us to be expertly crafted treasures that manifest the brilliant creativity of God.

---

30. Luther, "Freedom," 297.
31. Gen 1:27, 31 CEB; Ps 139:14.

Backstory Five—Theological Education as a Nursery of the Church

Because of its reliance on the individualistic and compartmental-ized style of education characteristic of the University of Berlin, theologians frequently critique the church but have been unable to gain the trust of church leaders. Consequently, the theological academy has often failed to address many of the wider problems of the church; and indeed, the academy has sometimes contrib-uted to those problems.[32] Theological schools and churches work within mutually exclusive bubbles.

By contrast, Philipp Spener, in addition to urging theological academies to be workshops of the Holy Spirit, implored schools to be "nurseries of the church for all estates."[33] To what was Spener referring? What would it mean for a Christian college, seminary, or divinity school to be a nursery of the church for all estates?

A nursery is a place in which things are nurtured. Spener un-derstood that theological students need to be cultivated. They're like young plants that are nurtured in growth. Years ago, it used to be that schools received theological students who'd already been discipled by their congregations, like partially grown plants. In that situation, the only thing schools needed to do was to prune and water the plants. The task of theological education was to shape and direct the religious knowledge of students. But now, some theological students know very little about the church, and students in theological academies often start their study as begin-ners in the faith, as spiritual seedlings. These unformed plant-ings, dispatched into ministry, may be sent into churches for the first time. This reality about the student body makeup at today's Christian colleges and seminaries means that rather than prun-ing plants that have already developed, professors are expected to

32. Dr. Willie James Jennings of Yale Divinity School narrates how the corrosive effects of the theological academy's white, Western individualism negatively affects the church in the US. See Jennings, *After Whiteness*.

33. Spener, *Pia Desideria*, 103.

foster the faith of relatively undeveloped seeds—faith that needs to be handled carefully and prudently.

If the plants in the nursery (students in theological schools) have changed across the centuries, the church for which we're preparing the plants has also changed. Neither theological schools nor denominational institutions seem to understand the complexities and challenges facing most congregations and parishes today. But the future of theological education is inextricably tied to the future of the church. The academy needs the church. Theological education isn't an end in itself; it exists as a vehicle for renewing the church. This was the point of Spener's whole agenda. The academy has sometimes been a place of deformation, but now we have an opportunity to make it a place of spiritual and intellectual flourishing for the sake of the church's health.

The theological academy needs the church, but the church of the future, for which the academy is training leaders, is being transformed into something that looks unlike its current configuration. In some parts of the country, profound changes have already occurred among congregations. Megachurches are declining. House churches and other smaller, experimental faith groups are prospering. Growth is taking place most prominently among congregations of color.

Since the church is changing, the future of theological education will look very different from before. Students, theological schools, and their placement settings must be willing to be risk takers and to engage in education in new ways. Christian colleges and seminaries have the chance to be dynamic colearners with the church in the emerging world. Students, faculty, programs, and institutions have the privilege of being humble learners, invited as guests into new spaces of ministry. Cross-disciplinary coeducators will exhibit ministerial relevance and the revival of spiritual leadership. Entrepreneurial ministry and the development of vocational skills will extend beyond the standard subjects previously covered in theological higher education. Students will learn to be comfortable with disruptive innovations and skunkworks that may fail.

The church also needs the academy. Theological education should provide intellectual and theological leadership for the broader Christian culture. We need the best minds to address ethical issues from biblical, historical, and theological angles in arenas such as bioethics, artificial intelligence, climate change, gender, race, sexuality, and interfaith communication. We must use the broad expertise of the university in order to have the most broadly educated students. The church of the future needs ministerial leaders who display intellectual rigor, deep and abiding spiritual formation, and liberative praxis in day-to-day ministry. Such an integration won't privilege any of these three components. It will equally emphasize the training of head, heart, and hands.

Spener said that theological schools will be nurseries of the church "for all estates." The late medieval idea of the structure of society was based on distinct estates. The word *estate* designated a great variety of social orders—structures such as class, gender, occupation, and position in society. Many people have heard of the "three estates," or classes, of the French realm, but the concept of an estate could extend to every social function and every profession, including the craft trades.[34]

By saying that theological academies will train students for the church of all estates, Spener declared that schools should educate folks for a church that exists without discrimination or prejudice, without separation into human-made classes or divisions. No matter one's background, all should be welcome. Spener decried the class segmentations of his day; four centuries later, we still haven't been able to form a church that is open to all estates. May our theological schools be places of hospitality for everyone, so that we're preparing students to serve a church that cherishes all people.

34. Huizinga, *Waning*, 57–58.

Bibliography

Anderson, Ray S. "Making the Transition: From a Theology of Ministry to a Ministry of Theology." In *From Midterms to Ministry: Practical Theologians on Pastoral Beginnings*, edited by Allan Hugh Cole Jr., 27–38. Grand Rapids, MI: Eerdmans, 2008.

Barnhart, Robert K., ed. *Chambers' Dictionary of Etymology*. New York: Chambers Harrap, 1988.

Barth, Karl. *Church Dogmatics*. Vol. 1.2, *The Doctrine of the Word of God*. Translated by G. T. Thomson and Harold Knight. Edited by G. W. Bromiley and T. F. Torrance. Edinburgh: T. and T. Clark, 1956.

Barton, Ruth Hailey. *Sacred Rhythms: Arranging Our Lives for Spiritual Transformation*. Downers Grove, IL: InterVarsity, 2006.

Bass, Dorothy C., and Susan R. Briehl, eds. *On Our Way: Christian Practices for Living a Whole Life*. Nashville: Upper Room, 2009.

Baum, Wilhelm, et al., eds. *Ioannis Calvini, Opera Quae Supersunt Omnia*. Corpus Reformatorum 29–87. Braunschweig, Germany: Schwetschke, 1863–1900.

Bittner, Vanessa, trans. *Masterpieces of the Tretyakov Gallery*. Moscow: The State Tretyakov Gallery, 1994.

Bock, Darrell, and Greg Forster. "Challenges to the Faith and Work Movement." *The Table Podcast*, Dallas Theological Seminary, October 27, 2015. Episode transcript, https://voice.dts.edu/tablepodcast/challenges-to-faith-and-work-movement/.

Bonhoeffer, Dietrich. *Life Together: The Classic Exploration of Christian Community*. 1939. Translated by John W. Doberstein. New York: HarperCollins, 1954.

Boulton, Matthew Myer. "Study." In *On Our Way: Christian Practices for Living a Whole Life*, edited by Dorothy C. Bass and Susan R. Briehl, 19–35. Nashville: Upper Room, 2009.

Brewer, LaPrincess C., et al. "Emergency Preparedness and Risk Communication among African American Churches: Leveraging a Community-Based

Bibliography

Participatory Research Partnership COVID-19 Initiative." *Preventing Chronic Disease* 17 (2020) e158. http://dx.doi.org/10.5888/pcd17.200408.

Buechner, Frederick. *Wishful Thinking: A Seeker's ABC*, rev. ed. London: Mowbray, 1993. Originally published as *Wishful Thinking: A Theological ABC* (New York: Harper and Row, 1973).

Chariton, Igumen, and Timothy Ware, eds. *The Art of Prayer: An Orthodox Anthology.* Translated by E. Kadloubovsky and E. M. Palmer. New York: Farrar, Straus, and Giroux, 1966.

Chilcote, Paul Wesley. *Recapturing the Wesleys' Vision: An Introduction to the Faith of John and Charles Wesley.* Downers Grove, IL: InterVarsity, 2004.

"Chronogical List of the Doctors of the Church." *U.S. Catholic* online, July 28, 2008. https://uscatholic.org/articles/200807/chronological-list-of-the-doctors-of-the-church/#.

Cillizza, Chris. "Millennials Don't Trust Anyone. That's a Big Deal." *Washington Post*, April 30, 2015.

Cook, Guillermo. *The Expectation of the Poor: Latin American Base Ecclesial Communities in Protestant Perspective.* Ossining, NY: Orbis, 1985.

Crawford, Evans E. *The Hum: Call and Response in African American Preaching.* Nashville: Abingdon, 1995.

Crowston, Clare. "Women, Gender, and Guilds in Early Modern Europe: An Overview of Recent Research." *International Review of Social History* 53, no. S16 (December 2008) 19–44. http://www.doi.org/10.1017/S0020859008003593.

Dayton, Donald W., and Douglas M. Strong. *Rediscovering an Evangelical Heritage: A Tradition and Trajectory of Integrating Piety and Justice.* Grand Rapids, MI: Baker Academic, 2014.

Dostoyevsky, Fyodor. *The Brothers Karamazov.* 1879–80. Translated by Constance Garnett. New York: Random House, 1950.

Ekblad, Bob. *Reading the Bible with the Damned.* Louisville: Westminster John Knox, 2005.

Epstein, Steven A. *Wage Labor and Guilds in Medieval Europe.* Chapel Hill: University of North Carolina Press, 2010.

Ferrari Lake Forest. "What Does Ferrari Mean?" https://www.ferrarilakeforest.com/manufacturer-information/what-does-ferrari-mean/.

Foster, Richard J. *Celebration of Discipline: The Path to Spiritual Growth.* 1978. New York: Harper One, 1998.

Gausepohl, Shannon. "Embracing 'Startup Culture' at Any Business Size." *Business News Daily*, May 26, 2016. https://www.businessnewsdaily.com/8379-embrace-startup-culture.html.

González, Justo L. *The History of Theological Education.* Nashville: Abingdon, 2015.

Gutiérrez, Gustavo. *We Drink from Our Own Wells: The Spiritual Journey of a People.* London: SCM, 2005.

Bibliography

Haines, Anna. "Asset-Based Community Development." In *An Introduction to Community Development*, 2nd ed., edited by Rhonda Phillips and Robert H. Pittman, 45–56. New York: Routledge, 2015.

Hambrick-Stowe, Charles E. *The Practice of Piety: Puritan Devotional Disciplines in Seventeenth-Century New England*. Chapel Hill: University of North Carolina Press, 1982.

Harper, Steve. *The Way to Heaven: The Gospel according to John Wesley*. Grand Rapids, MI: Zondervan, 2003.

Hernández, Arelis R., et al. "Federal Immigration Raids Net Many Without Criminal Records, Sowing Fear." *Washington Post*, February 16, 2017. https://www.washingtonpost.com/national/federal-immigration-raids-net-many-without-criminal-records-sowing-fear/2017/02/16/a37e5e76-f486-11e6-a9b0-ecee7ce475fc_story.html.

Hess, Lisa M. *Artisanal Theology: Intentional Formation in Radically Covenantal Companionship*. Eugene, OR: Cascade, 2009.

Hilbrands, Walter. "'With Psalms and Hymns': The Reformation, Music, and Liturgy." In *The Reformation: Its Roots and Its Legacy*, edited by Pierre Berthoud and Pieter J. Lalleman, 55–73. Eugene, OR: Wipf and Stock, 2017.

Hollister, C. Warren. *Medieval Europe: A Short History*. 8th ed. New York: McGraw-Hill, 1998.

Hudson, Hugh, dir. *Chariots of Fire*. 1982. Warner Bros. Pictures, Ladd Company, Allied Stars, Goldcrest Films, Enigma Productions. Amazon Prime Video. https://www.amazon.com/gp/video/detail/BoooIoQ2NQ/ref=atv_dp_share_cu_r.

Huizinga, J. *The Waning of the Middle Ages*. Garden City, NY: Anchor, 1954.

Irvin, Dale T., and Scott W. Sunquist. *History of the World Christian Movement*. Vol. 1, *Earliest Christianity to 1453*. Maryknoll, NY: Orbis, 2001.

Jennings, Willie James. *After Whiteness: An Education in Belonging*. Grand Rapids, MI: Eerdmans, 2020.

Johnson, Marissa J. "A Good Day to Die: A Black Good Friday Reflection." Medium.com, March 25, 2016. https://medium.com/@rissaoftheway/a-good-day-to-die-3cd5f02f94a2.

Jones, L. Gregory, and Susan Pendleton Jones. "Leadership, Pastoral Identity, and Friendship: Navigating the Transition from Seminary to the Parish." In *From Midterms to Ministry: Practical Theologians on Pastoral Beginnings*, edited by Allan Hugh Cole Jr., 13–26. Grand Rapids, MI: Eerdmans, 2008.

Kent, Keri Wyatt. "Collaborative Leadership." *Christianity Today*, Womenleaders.com blog, March 15, 2012. https://www.christianitytoday.com/women-leaders/2012/march/collaborative-leadership.html.

Kincannon, Keary C. "Home." Rising Hope United Methodist Mission Church online. https://risinghopesite.wordpress.com, predecessor website to https://risinghopeumc.org.

King, Martin Luther, Jr. *Why We Can't Wait*. New York: The New American Library, 1964.

Bibliography

Leach, Tara Beth. *Emboldened: A Vision for Empowering Women in Ministry.* Downers Grove, IL: InterVarsity, 2017.

Lindman, Janey Moore. "Beyond the Meetinghouse: Women and Protestant Spirituality in Early America." In *The Religious History of American Women: Reimagining the Past,* edited by Catherine A. Brekus, 142–60. Chapel Hill: University of North Carolina Press, 2007.

Loder, James E. *The Transforming Moment: Understanding Convictional Experiences.* San Francisco: Harper and Row, 1981.

Luther, Martin. "Freedom of a Christian." Translated by W. A. Lambert. In *Three Treatises,* 262–316. Philadelphia: Fortress, 1970.

McNeil, Brenda Salter. *Becoming Brave: Finding the Courage to Pursue Racial Justice Now.* Grand Rapids, MI: Brazos, 2020.

———. *Roadmap to Reconciliation 2.0: Moving Communities into Unity, Wholeness, and Justice.* Downers Grove, IL: InterVarsity, 2020. Rev. ed. of *Roadmap to Reconciliation: Moving Communities into Unity, Wholeness, and Justice* (Downers Grove, IL: InterVarsity, 2015).

Methodist Le Bonheur Healthcare. "Center of Excellence in Faith and Health." https://www.methodisthealth.org/about-us/faith-and-health/.

Miller, David W. *God at Work: The History and Promise of the Faith at Work Movement.* New York: Oxford University Press, 2007. https://doi.org/10.1093/acprof:oso/9780195314809.003.0008.

Mulholland, M. Robert, Jr. *Invitation to a Journey: A Road Map for Spiritual Formation.* Downers Grove, IL: InterVarsity, 2016.

Niebuhr, H. Richard. *Christ and Culture.* New York: HarperCollins, 2001.

Nietzche, Friedrich. *Beyond Good and Evil: Prelude to a Philosophy of the Future.* Translated by Helen Zimmern. London: Macmillan, 1907.

Nouwen, Henri J. M. *In the Name of Jesus.* New York: Crossroad, 1989.

———. *The Way of the Heart: The Spirituality of the Desert Fathers and Mothers.* New York: HarperCollins, 1981. Rev. reprint, New York: Ballantine, 2003.

Nouwen, Henri J. M., et al. *Compassion: A Reflection on the Christian Life.* New York: Image Doubleday, 1983.

Paulus, Michael. "Forms of Creation." Digital Wisdom, Patheos.com, December 6, 2018. www.patheos.com/blogs/digitalwisdom/2018/12/forms-of-creation/.

Peterson, Eugene H. *Five Smooth Stones for Pastoral Work.* Grand Rapids, MI: Eerdmans, 1980.

———. *A Long Obedience in the Same Direction: Discipleship in an Instant Society.* 1980. Downers Grove, IL: InterVarsity, 2000.

———. *The Pastor: A Memoir.* New York: HarperCollins, 2011.

———. *Under the Unpredictable Plant: An Exploration in Vocational Holiness.* Grand Rapids, MI: Eerdmans, 1992.

Rohr, Richard. "The Edge of the Inside." Center for Action and Contemplation online, September 12, 2017. https://cac.org/daily-meditations/the-edge-of-the-inside-2019-07-09/.

Bibliography

Scandrette, Mark. *Practicing the Way of Jesus: Life Together in the Kingdom of Love.* Downers Grove, IL: InterVarsity, 2011.

Smith, C. Christopher, and John Pattison. *Slow Church: Cultivating Community in the Patient Way of Jesus.* Downers Grove, IL: InterVarsity, 2014.

Spener, Philip Jacob. *Pia Desideria.* 1675. Edited and translated by Theodore G. Tappert. Philadelphia: Fortress, 1964.

Spink, Kathryn. *Mother Teresa: A Complete Authorized Biography.* New York: HarperCollins, 1997.

Stein, K. James. *Philipp Jakob Spener: Pietist Patriarch.* Chicago: Covenant, 1986.

Taylor, Charles. *A Secular Age.* Cambridge: Harvard University Press, 2007.

Teresa, Mother. *Come Be My Light: The Private Writings of the Saint of Calcutta.* Edited by Brian Kolodiejchuk. New York: Doubleday Religion, 2007.

————. *My Life for the Poor.* Edited by José Luis González-Balado and Janet N. Playfoot. San Francisco: Harper and Row, 1985.

Teresa of Ávila. *The Life of Saint Teresa of Ávila by Herself.* 1611. Translated by J. M. Cohen. London: Penguin, 1957.

Teresa of Calcutta. *Mother Teresa: A Simple Path.* Edited by Lucinda Vardey. New York: Ballantine, 1995.

Thielicke, Helmut. *A Little Exercise for Young Theologians.* Grand Rapids, MI: Eerdmans, 2016.

Thompson, Marjorie J. *Soul Feast: An Invitation to the Christian Spiritual Life.* Louisville: Westminster John Knox, 1995.

Thurman, Howard. *For the Inward Journey: The Writings of Howard Thurman.* Edited by Anne Spencer Thurman. New York: Harcourt Brace Jovanovich, 1984.

————. *Jesus and the Disinherited.* Boston: Beacon, 1976.

Tocqueville, Alexis de. *Democracy in America.* 1831.

Trotter, Lilias. Diary, unpublished. In "Quotes from the Writings of Lilias Trotter," Lilias Trotter Legacy online, https://liliastrotter.com/quotes/. Information verified in Kimberly Wood, Lilias Trotter Legacy, email correspondence, October 28, 2021.

Turkle, Sheri. "Always-On/Always-On-You: The Tethered Self." In *Handbook of Mobile Communication Studies,* edited by James E. Katz, 121–38. Cambridge: MIT Press, 2008. http://dx.doi.org/10.7551/mitpress/9780262113120.001.0001.

Vallet, Ronald E. *Stewards of the Gospel: Reforming Theological Education.* Grand Rapids, MI: Eerdmans, 2011.

Vaters, Karl. "Forget Being Culturally Relevant—The Church Needs to Be Contextually Real." *Christianity Today,* Pivot blog, March 30, 2016. https://www.christianitytoday.com/karl-vaters/2016/march/forget-being-culturally-relevant-church-needs-to-be-context.html.

Waber, Ben, et al. "Workspaces That Move People." *Harvard Business Review,* October 2014. https://hbr.org/2014/10/workspaces-that-move-people.

Bibliography

Weems, Renita J. *Listening for God: A Minister's Journey through Silence and Doubt*. New York: Simon and Schuster, 1999.

Wesley, Charles. *Hymns for Children, and Others of Riper Years*. Bristol, UK: William Pine, 1768.

Wesley, John. *John Wesley*. Edited by Albert C. Outler. New York: Oxford University Press, 1964.

———. "The Means of Grace." 1746. In vol. 5 of *The Works of John Wesley*, 3rd ed., 185–201. Grand Rapids, MI: Baker, 1996.

———. *The Methodist Societies 1: History, Nature, and Design*. Edited by Ruper E. Davies. 1989. Vol. 9 in *The Bicentennial Edition of the Works of John Wesley*, edited by Frank Baker and Richard P. Heitzenrater. 35 vols. Nashville, TN: Abingdon, 1984–.

———. *The Works of John Wesley*. 3rd ed. Grand Rapids, MI: Baker, 1996.

White, James F. *Introduction to Christian Worship*. 3rd ed. Nashville: Abingdon, 2000.

Wirzba, Norman. *Living the Sabbath: Discovering the Rhythms of Rest and Delight*. Grand Rapids, MI: Brazos, 2006.

Wright, Dana R., and John D. Kuentzel, eds. *Redemptive Transformation in Practical Theology*. Grand Rapids, MI: Eerdmans, 2004.

Wright, N. T. *Surprised by Hope: Rethinking Heaven, the Resurrection, and the Mission of the Church*. New York: HarperCollins, 2008.

CPSIA information can be obtained
at www.ICGtesting.com
Printed in the USA
JSHW071733251122
33809JS00004B/15